GoodFood

101 PASTA & NOODLE DISHES

First published 2005
Published by BBC Books,
an imprint of Ebury Publishing
A Random House Group company

Photographs © BBC Magazines 2005
Recipes © BBC Magazines 2005
Book design © Woodlands Books Ltd 2005
All recipes contained within this book first appeared in
BBC *Good Food* magazine.

The Random House Group Limited Reg. No. 954009

Addresses for companies within the Random House Group can be found
at www.randomhouse.co.uk

A CIP catalogue record for this book is available from the British Library

The Random House Group Limited supports The Forest Stewardship Council
(FSC), the leading international forest certification organization. All our titles that
are printed on Greenpeace approved FSC certified paper carry the FSC logo.
Our paper procurement policy can be found at
www.rbooks.co.uk/environment

To buy books by your favourite authors and register for offers visit
www.rbooks.co.uk

Printed and bound by Firmengruppe APPL, aprinta druck, Wemding, Germany

Commissioning Editor: Vivien Bowler
Project Editor: Sarah Reece
Project Co-ordinator for *BBC Good Food Magazine*: Sarah Sysum
Designer: Kathryn Gammon
Production: Peter Hunt

ISBN: 9780563522201

20 19 18 17 16 15 14 13 12

GoodFood

101 PASTA & NOODLE DISHES
TRIED-AND-TESTED RECIPES

Editor
Jeni Wright

BBC
BOOKS

Contents

Introduction   6

Introduction

At BBC *Good Food* magazine we don't know anyone who doesn't like pasta and noodles – and we bet you don't either! So versatile, so quick and so healthy, they're the ultimate convenience foods. Whether you're cooking a simple after-work supper in a hurry, entertaining friends on a Saturday night, or spending a leisurely afternoon cooking up a storm, you'll find over 100 pasta and noodle recipes to choose from in this collection, each one tried and tested in the *Good Food* kitchen.

There's something for everybody, including recipes exclusively for vegetarians – try our *Tricolore Tagliatelle*, pictured opposite (see page 110 for recipe) – and a selection of low-fat dishes that don't sacrifice flavour for the sake of lean cuisine. In fact every recipe comes calorie counted with a full breakdown of essential nutrients and at-a-glance information to help you plan healthy, well-balanced meals.

So pop this book in your bag when you go to the shops. Instant inspiration guaranteed.

Jeni Wright
BBC *Good Food* magazine

Conversion tables

NOTES ON THE RECIPES
• Eggs are medium in the UK and Australia (large in America) unless stated otherwise.
• Wash all fresh produce before preparation.

OVEN TEMPERATURES

Gas	°C	Fan °C	°F	Oven temp.
¼	110	90	225	Very cool
½	120	100	250	Very cool
1	140	120	275	Cool or slow
2	150	130	300	Cool or slow
3	160	140	325	Warm
4	180	160	350	Moderate
5	190	170	375	Moderately hot
6	200	180	400	Fairly hot
7	220	200	425	Hot
8	230	210	450	Very hot
9	240	220	475	Very hot

APPROXIMATE WEIGHT CONVERSIONS
• All the recipes in this book list both imperial and metric measurements. Conversions are approximate and have been rounded up or down. Follow one set of measurements only; do not mix the two.
• Cup measurements, which are used by cooks in Australia and America, have not been listed here as they vary from ingredient to ingredient. Please use kitchen scales to measure dry/solid ingredients.

SPOON MEASURES

• Spoon measurements are level unless otherwise specified.

• 1 teaspoon = 5ml

• 1 tablespoon = 15ml

• 1 Australian tablespoon = 20ml (cooks in Australia should measure 3 teaspoons where 1 tablespoon is specified in a recipe)

APPROXIMATE LIQUID CONVERSIONS

metric	imperial	AUS	US
50ml	2fl oz	¼ cup	¼ cup
125ml	4fl oz	½ cup	½ cup
175ml	6fl oz	¾ cup	¾ cup
225ml	8fl oz	1 cup	1 cup
300ml	10fl oz/½ pint	½ pint	1¼ cups
450ml	16fl oz	2 cups	2 cups/1 pint
600ml	20fl oz/1 pint	1 pint	2½ cups
1 litre	35fl oz/1¾ pints	1¾ pints	1 quart

This amazingly quick and tasty dish works well with fresh salmon, too. Just cook for 3 minutes on each side and leave out the bacon.

Chicken with Creamy Bacon Penne

1 tbsp olive oil
2 boneless skinless chicken breasts
100g/4oz smoked lardons
(chopped bacon)
4 tbsp dry white wine
100g/4oz frozen petits pois
5 tbsp double cream
220g pack 'instant' cooked penne

Takes 10 minutes • Serves 2

1 Heat the oil in a deep non-stick frying pan, add the chicken and scatter with the lardons. Leave to cook over a high heat for 4 minutes.
2 Turn the chicken over in the pan, give the lardons a stir, then pour in the wine and let it bubble over a high heat until it has virtually evaporated.
3 Now add the peas, cream and penne, season and stir well. Cover the pan and cook for 4 minutes more until the chicken is cooked all the way through. Serve straight away.

• Per serving 639 kcalories, protein 48g, carbohydrate 24g, fat 38g, saturated fat 17g, fibre 3g, added sugar none, salt 1.86g

Adapt this tasty and substantial winter soup according to what you've got in the freezer – try adding frozen broad beans, sweetcorn or spinach.

Storecupboard Minestrone

2 tbsp olive oil
1 onion, roughly chopped
2 × 400g cans chopped tomatoes
1 tbsp vegetable bouillon powder
1 tbsp pesto, plus extra to serve
pinch of sugar
50g/2oz dried mini pasta shapes
for soup (such as farfalline),
or spaghetti or other pasta,
broken into small pieces
420g can mixed pulses, drained
and rinsed
200g/8oz frozen green vegetables,
such as sliced green beans
and peas

Takes 30 minutes • Serves 2

1 Heat the oil in a large saucepan and cook the onion over a low heat until softened. Pour in the tomatoes and 4 canfuls of water. Sprinkle in the bouillon powder, then stir in the pesto, sugar and seasoning to taste.
2 Increase the heat and bring to the boil. Add the pasta and simmer for 10 minutes or until just tender, stirring occasionally.
3 Tip in the pulses and frozen vegetables, stir well and bring to the boil again. Cover and simmer for 10 minutes, stirring occasionally. Taste for seasoning. Serve with extra pesto.

• Per serving 256 kcalories, protein 12g, carbohydrate 33g, fat 9g, saturated fat 2g, fibre 9g, added sugar 1g, salt 2.16g

This simple Italian dish with a kick is perfect for entertaining
if you're short of time.

Conchiglie with Tomato Sauce

2 tbsp extra virgin olive oil
2 garlic cloves, chopped
300ml/½ pint good-quality tomato passata
500g pack conchiglie (shells) or other short pasta shapes
50g/2oz butter
1 tbsp crushed black pepper
100ml/3½fl oz single cream
small handful of fresh basil leaves, roughly torn
2 tbsp vodka (optional)
3 tbsp freshly grated parmesan cheese

Takes 20 minutes • Serves 6

1 Heat the oil in a small saucepan and fry the garlic gently until golden. Stir in the passata, season and simmer for 10 minutes.
2 While the sauce is cooking, boil the pasta in salted water according to the packet instructions. Drain well.
3 Melt the butter in a large saucepan, add the pasta and black pepper and toss well until the pasta is coated. With the heat high, continue tossing the pasta while adding the tomato sauce, cream and basil. Stir in the vodka, if using. Serve straight away, sprinkled with the parmesan.

• Per serving 476 kcalories, protein 13g, carbohydrate 69g, fat 17g, saturated fat 8g, fibre 3g, added sugar 1g, salt 0.6g

A clever, luxurious supper idea – the ultimate comfort food.

Spaghetti with Mascarpone and Rocket

200g/8oz spaghetti
85g bag rocket
½ × 250g tub mascarpone cheese
2 heaped tbsp pesto
25g/1oz parmesan cheese,
freshly grated

Takes 20 minutes • Serves 2

1 Cook the spaghetti in a large pan of salted boiling water for 10–12 minutes, or according to the packet instructions, until tender.
2 Meanwhile, chop about half of the rocket and mix in a large bowl with about three quarters of the mascarpone, the pesto and plenty of black pepper.
3 Drain the spaghetti, reserving some of the water. Toss the spaghetti into the mascarpone mixture until coated, loosening it with a few tablespoons of the water, then add the remaining rocket and mascarpone and toss just once to mix lightly. Serve in warmed bowls, topped with parmesan.

• Per serving 800 kcalories, protein 27g, carbohydrate 79g, fat 44g, saturated fat 24.5g, fibre 3.8g, added sugar none, salt 0.84g

Turn a bag of salad and some pasta shapes into a quick
and interesting midweek meal.

Watercress and Melting Brie Pasta

500g pack short pasta shapes,
such as egg riccioli
2 tbsp extra virgin olive oil,
plus extra to serve
2 tsp chilli purée
200g/8oz brie cheese, diced
12 sun-blush tomatoes, halved
120g bag mixed spinach, watercress
and rocket

Takes 15 minutes • Serves 4

1 Cook the pasta in a large pan of salted boiling water according to the packet instructions, until tender. Drain and return to the pan. Blend the olive oil with the chilli purée and stir into the pasta with the brie, tomatoes and seasoning. Stir until the cheese starts to melt.
2 Divide the pasta between four warmed bowls and top each with a quarter of the mixed leaves. Sprinkle with olive oil and grind black pepper over the top.

• Per serving 693 kcalories, protein 26g, carbohydrate 99g, fat 24g, saturated fat 9.9g, fibre 5.2g, added sugar none, salt 1.13g

This is a simple and healthy pasta dish that's perfect
for all the family.

Rigatoni with Pesto Chicken

100g/4oz rigatoni or penne
100g/4oz young leaf spinach,
washed
2 tbsp pesto
1 tsp olive oil
2 cooked chicken breasts, skinned
and cut into chunky strips
85g/3oz cherry tomatoes, halved
freshly grated parmesan cheese,
to serve

Takes 15 minutes • Serves 2

1 Cook the pasta in a large pan of salted boiling water for 8–10 minutes, or according to the packet instructions, until tender.
2 Stir the spinach in with the pasta for the last minute, then drain well and toss with the pesto, olive oil, chicken and tomatoes.
3 Season to taste and serve straight away, sprinkled with parmesan.

• Per serving 448 kcalories, protein 49g, carbohydrate 40g, fat 11g, saturated fat 3.5g, fibre 3.1g, added sugar none, salt 0.58g

A cheap and easy supper made from readily available ingredients.

Leek, Pea and Ham Pasta

300g/10oz spaghetti
175g/6oz frozen peas
25g/1oz butter
1 large leek
4 eggs
140g/5oz thick slice of smoked ham,
cut into cubes
85g/3oz cheddar or Lancashire
cheese, grated

Takes 15 minutes • Serves 4

1 Bring a large pan of salted water to the boil. Add the spaghetti and cook for about 10–12 minutes, adding the peas for the last 3 minutes of the cooking time.
2 Meanwhile, heat the butter in a small pan. Wash and slice the leek. Add to the pan and cook over a medium heat for 3 minutes until softened.
3 Beat the eggs in a bowl and season. Drain the pasta and immediately return to the pan. Tip in the leeks, eggs, ham and half the cheese. Stir well. Adjust the seasoning and serve sprinkled with the remaining cheese.

• Per serving 553 kcalories, protein 32g, carbohydrate 61g, fat 22g, saturated fat 10g, fibre 6g, added sugar none, salt 1.67g

An impressive and quick light meal that's big on flavour but short on ingredients.

Penne with Tuna and Parsley

400g/14oz penne
2 × 200g cans tuna in olive oil
4 tbsp vinaigrette dressing
1 fresh red chilli, seeded and finely chopped
2 garlic cloves, finely chopped
1 large bunch of parsley, finely chopped

Takes 20 minutes • Serves 4

1 Cook the penne in a large pan of salted boiling water for 8–10 minutes, or according to the packet instructions, until tender.
2 Meanwhile, drain the oil from the tuna into a small pan, spoon in the vinaigrette and add the chilli and garlic. Heat gently, just to warm through, then pour into a warmed large bowl. Flake the tuna into large chunks with a fork and toss in the warm dressing.
3 Drain the pasta and tip into the bowl. Toss gently to mix and sprinkle liberally with the parsley and some black pepper – the heat of the pasta will warm the tuna and parsley through. Serve immediately.

• Per serving 779 kcalories, protein 34g, carbohydrate 77g, fat 39g, saturated fat 6g, fibre 3.4g, added sugar 0.2g, salt 0.74g

A few spoonfuls of pasta water added to the sauce is the magic ingredient in this delicious, creamy version of a true Italian classic.

Spaghetti Carbonara

350g/12oz spaghetti
50g/2oz unsalted butter
100g/4oz pancetta (without rind),
finely chopped
2 plump garlic cloves, squashed
50g/2oz pecorino cheese,
freshly grated
50g/2oz parmesan cheese,
freshly grated
3 large eggs, beaten

Takes 30 minutes • Serves 4

1 Cook the spaghetti according to the packet instructions until just tender. Meanwhile, melt the butter in a large wide frying pan, tip in the pancetta and garlic and cook on a medium heat for 5 minutes until the pancetta is golden and crisp. Turn the heat down low and discard the garlic.

2 When the spaghetti is ready, lift it out of the water with tongs and put it in the pan with the pancetta. Leave the pasta water in its pan.

3 Mix most of the cheese with the eggs and seasoning. Off the heat, mix the eggs and cheese into the spaghetti, adding a few spoonfuls of pasta water to make it saucy. Serve sprinkled with black pepper and the remaining cheese.

• Per serving 655 kcalories, protein 32g, carbohydrate 66g, fat 31g, saturated fat 16g, fibre 3g, added sugar none, salt 2.02g

This hearty dish tastes great cold,
so pack any leftovers into your lunchbox.

Sizzled Sausage Pasta

400g/14oz short pasta shapes,
such as trompetti
6 good-quality sausages
140g/5oz sun-dried tomatoes
4 tbsp oil from the sun-dried
tomato jar
generous handful of parsley,
coarsely chopped

Takes 25 minutes • Serves 4

1 Cook the pasta in a large pan of salted boiling water for 8–10 minutes, or according to the packet instructions, until tender.
2 Meanwhile, peel the skins off the sausages and chop the meat into small pieces. Chop the tomatoes into small chunks. Heat 1 tablespoon of the tomato oil in a large, deep frying pan or wok and sizzle the sausage chunks for 6–8 minutes until crumbly and golden. Stir in the tomato chunks and the remaining oil, then heat through.
3 Drain the pasta well and toss into the sausage mixture with the parsley. Season, make sure everything is well mixed and serve straight from the pan.

• Per serving 775 kcalories, protein 28g, carbohydrate 86g, fat 38g, saturated fat 10g, fibre 5g, added sugar none, salt 3.24g

Short pasta shapes are good for serving with this delicious sauce, as it gets trapped inside.

Creamy Pasta with Crispy Bacon

200g/8oz short pasta shapes, such as trompetti, conchiglie or penne
85g/3oz frozen peas
4 back bacon rashers
25g/1oz butter
1 small onion, finely chopped
142ml carton whipping or double cream
20g pack flatleaf parsley, roughly chopped

Takes 25 minutes • Serves 2

1 Cook the pasta in a large pan of salted boiling water for 8–10 minutes, or according to the packet instructions, until tender. Add the peas to the pasta for the last 3 minutes.
2 While the pasta is cooking, grill the bacon until crisp, then snip into strips with scissors. Melt the butter in a pan and fry the onion over a medium heat for about 5 minutes until soft and golden. Pour in the cream, season and simmer until thickened slightly.
3 Drain the pasta and peas, reserving some of the water, then return to the pan and pour in the sauce. Toss well to mix, adding some of the water if the sauce is too thick. Toss in the parsley and bacon, taste for seasoning and serve straight away.

• Per serving 911 kcalories, protein 25g, carbohydrate 84g, fat 55g, saturated fat 30.1g, fibre 6.2g, added sugar none, salt 1.92g

Use 100g/4oz frozen peas instead of the courgettes,
if you prefer.

Home-from-work Spaghetti

400g/14oz spaghetti
2 tbsp olive oil
4 streaky bacon rashers, chopped
2 courgettes, chopped
250g pack cherry tomatoes, halved
4 tbsp pesto
freshly grated parmesan cheese,
to serve

Takes 20 minutes • Serves 4

1 Cook the spaghetti in a large pan of salted boiling water for 10–12 minutes, or according to the packet instructions, until tender.
2 Meanwhile, heat the oil in a large, deep frying pan and fry the bacon for 5 minutes until it starts to crisp. Tip in the courgettes and tomatoes and cook for 2–3 minutes until the courgettes begin to brown round the edges and the tomatoes start to soften.
3 When the pasta is cooked, spoon a couple of tablespoons of the water into the vegetables, then drain the pasta and tip it into the vegetables too. Spoon in the pesto and toss until everything is coated. Serve with parmesan.

• Per serving 512 kcalories, protein 19g, carbohydrate 77g, fat 16g, saturated fat 4g, fibre 4g, added sugar none, salt 0.81g

No microwave? Cook the oil, lemon juice or vinegar, tomatoes and anchovies in a saucepan over a low heat for 3–4 minutes, stirring once.

Tuna Pasta Niçoise

350g/12oz short pasta shapes, such as conchiglie or penne
4 tbsp olive oil
1 tbsp lemon juice or white wine vinegar
250g pack cherry tomatoes, halved
50g can anchovy fillets, drained and chopped
80g can tuna in olive oil, drained
handful of fresh herbs, such as chives, basil, parsley

Takes 20 minutes • Serves 4

1 Cook the pasta in a large pan of salted boiling water for 8–10 minutes, or according to the packet instructions, until tender.
2 Meanwhile, put the oil and lemon juice or vinegar into a medium microwave-safe bowl. Tip in the tomatoes and anchovies and gently mix with the dressing. Microwave on high for 2–2½ minutes, stirring halfway through, until the tomatoes just start to burst and soften.
3 Drain the pasta and return it to the pan. Break the tuna into rough chunks, then toss into the pasta with the tomatoes and herbs. Season with black pepper and serve immediately.

• Per serving 474 kcalories, protein 18g, carbohydrate 68g, fat 16g, saturated fat 2g, fibre 3g, added sugar none, salt 0.94g

A quick, tasty and filling pasta dish –
just toss it together and serve.

Spaghetti with Chorizo

80g pack sliced chorizo sausage
good handful of flatleaf parsley
2 red peppers from a jar,
in brine or oil
300g/10oz fresh spaghetti
2 tbsp olive oil
50g/2oz parmesan cheese, freshly
grated, plus extra to serve

Takes 10 minutes • Serves 4

1 Put a pan of water on a high heat to boil. Meanwhile, snip the chorizo into strips with scissors and chop the parsley and red peppers.
2 When the water is boiling briskly, add the spaghetti with a good measure of salt, stir and return to the boil. Cook for 3 minutes.
3 In a large frying pan, heat the oil and add the chorizo, peppers and plenty of black pepper. Cook for a minute or so, until heated through and the juices are stained red from the paprika in the chorizo. Scoop half a mugful of pasta water from the pan, drain the remainder and tip the spaghetti into the frying pan.
4 Add the parsley and parmesan, toss well and splash in the pasta water, to moisten. Hand round extra parmesan at the table.

• Per serving 444 kcalories, protein 18g, carbohydrate 46g, fat 22g, saturated fat 6g, fibre 3g, added sugar none, salt 2.21g

Stuffed pasta comes in a wide variety of fillings – choose your favourite for this fantastically quick and tasty recipe.

10-minute Tortellini

250g pack fresh spinach and ricotta tortellini
1 tbsp olive oil
250g pack cherry tomatoes
2 × 20g packs parsley, leaves roughly chopped
3 tbsp finely grated parmesan cheese

Takes 5–10 minutes • Serves 2

1 Boil the pasta for 2 minutes until just cooked. Meanwhile, heat the oil in the frying pan and sizzle the tomatoes until they start to blister.
2 When the pasta is cooked, drain it quickly, reserving some cooking water. Put the tomatoes back on a high heat. Tip in the pasta, parsley, a splash of cooking water and most of the parmesan. Bubble everything together and season with black pepper and salt if you want. Serve with the remaining parmesan.

• Per serving 482 kcalories, protein 18g, carbohydrate 62g, fat 20g, saturated fat 8g, fibre 4g, added sugar none, salt 1.5g

Look for jars of Italian clams in tomato sauce in your local supermarket or any Italian deli.

Speedy Spaghetti with Clams

175g/6oz spaghetti
2 × 130g jars clams in tomato sauce
splash of wine, whatever you have
1 garlic clove, finely crushed
handful of parsley
freshly grated parmesan cheese,
to serve (optional)

Takes 15–20 minutes • Serves 2

1 Cook the spaghetti in a large pan of salted boiling water for 12 minutes, or according to the packet instructions, until tender.
2 Meanwhile, tip the clam sauce into a small pan, pour in the wine and add the garlic. Simmer for a few minutes while you coarsely chop the parsley, then stir it into the sauce and grind in a good amount of black pepper.
3 Drain the spaghetti and tip into a warmed bowl. Pour in the sauce and toss well. Serve at once, with grated parmesan scattered over if you like.

• Per serving 385 kcalories, protein 19g, carbohydrate 72g, fat 3g, saturated fat none, fibre 3g, added sugar none, salt 2.17g

Try to use dry-cure bacon as it is better for dry frying
and will give a crisper finish.

Spinach, Bacon and Pine Nut Pasta

finely grated zest of 1 lemon, plus
2 tbsp juice
3 tbsp olive oil, plus extra
for drizzling
300g/10oz pasta, such as
pappardelle
4 streaky bacon rashers,
cut into strips
50g/2oz pine nuts
225g bag baby leaf spinach,
thick stalks removed

Takes 25 minutes • Serves 4
(easily halved)

1 Mix the lemon zest and juice with the olive oil. Season and set aside. Cook the pasta in a large pan of salted boiling water for 10–12 minutes, or according to the packet instructions, until tender.
2 Meanwhile, heat a frying pan and dry fry the bacon until golden. Tip in the pine nuts and cook with the bacon until toasted golden.
3 Drain the pasta, return to the hot pan and tip in the spinach leaves, stirring gently until wilted. Toss in the bacon, pine nuts and lemon dressing. Season to taste, then serve drizzled with a little olive oil and sprinkled with black pepper.

• Per serving 495 kcalories, protein 16g, carbohydrate 59g, fat 23g, saturated fat 4g, fibre 4g, added sugar none, salt 0.86g

To make tossing the pasta a little easier, pour only half the sauce into the pan, then spoon the remaining sauce over the individual servings.

Linguine with Tuna Sauce

4 tbsp extra virgin olive oil
3 tbsp chopped fresh flatleaf parsley
2 garlic cloves, finely chopped
1 fresh red chilli, seeded and finely chopped
1cm/½in piece of fresh ginger, peeled and finely chopped
450g/1lb creamed tomatoes (passata)
2 × 200g cans tuna in olive oil, drained and flaked
375g/13oz linguine

Takes 30 minutes • Serves 4

1 Heat the oil in a medium pan. Toss in 2 tablespoons of the parsley, the garlic, chilli and ginger and fry for a few minutes until slightly soft. Tip in the tomatoes and cook for another few minutes. Fold in the tuna, season and simmer for 10 minutes.
2 Meanwhile, cook the pasta in a large pan of salted boiling water for 10–12 minutes, or according to the packet instructions, until tender.
3 Drain the pasta, then return it to the pan and pour in the sauce. Toss well, sprinkle over the remaining parsley and serve.

• Per serving 615 kcalories, protein 35g, carbohydrate 78g, fat 20g, saturated fat 3g, fibre 3g, added sugar 2g, salt 1.2g

Use cooked flaked salmon or white fish instead of the chicken, if you prefer.

Chicken Tarragon Pasta

250g/9oz pasta, such as pappardelle or tagliatelle
2 tbsp olive oil
2 boneless skinless chicken breasts, cut into small pieces
2 garlic cloves, chopped
142ml carton single cream
3 tbsp roughly chopped fresh tarragon leaves
100g/4oz spinach leaves, thick stalks removed
lemon wedges, to serve

Takes 30 minutes • Serves 3

1 Cook the pasta in a large pan of salted boiling water for 8–10 minutes, or according to the packet instructions, until tender.
2 Meanwhile, heat the oil in a large frying pan and fry the chicken over a high heat for 4–5 minutes, until golden and cooked. Add the garlic, cream, tarragon and 3 tablespoons of the pasta cooking water. Heat through gently.
3 When the pasta is cooked, stir in the spinach (it will wilt in the hot water). Drain the spinach and pasta well, then toss into the creamy chicken. Season and serve with lemon wedges.

• Per serving 560 kcalories, protein 35g, carbohydrate 65g, fat 19g, saturated fat 7g, fibre 3g, added sugar none, salt 0.58g

Serve this simple but impressive dish
with a crisp green salad.

Pork with Pappardelle

500g/1lb 2oz pork fillet, cut into
2cm/¾in-thick slices
seasoned flour, for coating
2 tbsp olive oil
300g/10oz pappardelle
25g/1oz pine nuts
grated zest of ½ lemon
juice of 1 lemon
1 tbp clear honey
good handful of flatleaf parsley,
chopped

Takes 25 minutes • Serves 4

1 Toss the pork in seasoned flour to coat very lightly. Shake off the excess. Heat 1 tablespoon of the oil in a large frying pan and fry the pork in a single layer until browned, about 3 minutes each side. Remove and keep warm.

2 Cook the pasta in a large pan of salted boiling water according to the packet instructions, until tender. Meanwhile, heat the remaining oil in the frying pan and fry the pine nuts until lightly browned. Stir in the lemon zest, juice and honey, then bubble briefly, stirring, to make a sauce.

3 Return the pork to the pan and scatter with the parsley. Cook for 3 minutes, turning the pork halfway through, until hot. Drain the pasta and serve with the pork.

• Per serving 566 kcalories, protein 38g, carbohydrate 64g, fat 19g, saturated fat 4.4g, fibre 2.7g, added sugar 2.9g, salt 0.44g

Create something special using
a storecupboard sauce.

Four Cheese Pasta Florentine

400g/14oz penne pasta
225g pack chestnut mushrooms,
thickly sliced
1 tsp olive oil
350g jar four cheese sauce
250g bag baby spinach leaves
25g/1oz walnut halves,
broken up roughly
50g/2oz blue cheese, crumbled

Takes 25 minutes • Serves 4

1 Turn on the grill. Cook the pasta in a large pan of salted boiling water for 10 minutes, or according to the packet instructions, until tender. Meanwhile, fry the mushrooms in the oil for 5 minutes until golden and softened.
2 Tip the four cheese sauce and spinach into the mushroom pan and heat through until the spinach wilts. Drain the pasta, stir into the sauce and season with pepper.
3 Tip into a large baking dish, sprinkle the walnuts over, then scatter the blue cheese on top. Grill for 5–8 minutes until the cheese bubbles.

• Per serving 639 kcalories, protein 24g, carbohydrate 83g, fat 25g, saturated fat 10g, fibre 6g, added sugar none, salt 1.31g

You can fry the breadcrumbs several hours ahead and, by the time the spaghetti has cooked, the remaining ingredients will be ready as well.

Spaghetti with Hot-smoked Salmon

125ml/4fl oz extra virgin olive oil
25g/1oz fresh white breadcrumbs
500g/1lb 2oz spaghetti
2 garlic cloves, very finely chopped
2 tiny dried bird's eye chillies, finely crumbled, or ¼ tsp chilli flakes
finely grated zest of 1 lemon
4 tbsp capers in brine, drained
85g/3oz rocket leaves
200g/8oz hot-smoked salmon, flaked

Takes 40 minutes • Serves 4–6

1 Heat 2 tablespoons of the oil in a small frying pan and fry the breadcrumbs over a medium heat for 3–4 minutes until golden and crisp, turning often. Tip into a small bowl.
2 Cook the pasta in plenty of salted boiling water for 10–12 minutes, or according to the packet instructions, until tender. Put the rest of the oil in a small pan with the garlic and chillies. Warm gently over a low heat so they flavour the oil – don't let the garlic fry.
3 Drain the pasta and tip it into a warmed very large serving bowl. Quickly add the lemon zest and capers to the oil, then pour over the pasta. Toss well, add the rocket and salmon and toss again, taking care not to break up the salmon too much. Scatter the breadcrumbs on top just before serving.

• Per serving for four 796 kcalories, protein 28g, carbohydrate 99g, fat 35g, saturated fat 5.3g, fibre 4.5g, added sugar none, salt 2.41g

Bolognese sauce is brilliant for making ahead – put it in a bowl, leave to cool, cover tightly with cling film and refrigerate for up to three days.

Classic Tagliatelle Bolognese

2 tbsp olive oil
1 medium onion, finely chopped
1 medium carrot, finely chopped
1 celery stick, finely chopped
2 garlic cloves, crushed
85g/3oz diced pancetta
250g/9oz minced beef
250g/9oz minced pork
300ml/½ pint full-fat milk
300ml/½ pint dry white or red wine
2 tbsp tomato purée
2 × 400g cans chopped tomatoes
2 tsp dried mixed herbs
350g/12oz tagliatelle
freshly grated parmesan cheese,
to serve

Takes about 2¾ hours • Serves 4–6

1 Heat the oil in a large pan and gently cook the chopped vegetables with the garlic and pancetta for 8–10 minutes. Add the meat and cook until browned, breaking up any lumps.
2 Pour in the milk and stir, then increase the heat and simmer for 10–15 minutes until the milk has almost disappeared. Repeat with the wine. Stir in the tomato purée, then pour in the tomatoes and 2 canfuls of water. Add the herbs and seasoning and bring to the boil, stirring, then turn down the heat to its lowest setting, half cover the pan and simmer very gently for 2 hours, stirring occasionally.
3 When the sauce is done, turn off the heat and let it stand while you cook the tagliatelle according to the packet instructions. Taste the sauce for seasoning before tossing with the pasta. Serve parmesan separately.

• Per serving for four 824 kcalories, protein 45g, carbohydrate 81g, fat 32g, saturated fat 11.9g, fibre 6.1g, added sugar none, salt 1.91g

Use home-grown or vine-ripened tomatoes for the sauce as an intense, sweet tomato flavour is at the heart of this dish.

Sicilian Lamb with Noodles

1 large onion, roughly chopped
2 fresh red chillies, seeded and roughly chopped
1kg/2lb 4oz ripe tomatoes, halved
2 red peppers, seeded and chopped
2 garlic cloves, peeled
5 tbsp olive oil
1kg/2lb 4oz lamb fillet, trimmed of fat and cut into 2cm/¾in slices
500g pack egg pappardelle
50g/2oz pine nuts, toasted
5 tbsp chopped fresh mint
2 tbsp chopped fresh parsley

Takes about 1 hour • Serves 6

1 Preheat the oven to 200°C/Gas 6/fan oven 180°C. Put the onion, chillies, tomatoes, peppers and garlic in a roasting tin. Drizzle with 2 tablespoons of the oil, season and roast for 25 minutes. Tip the vegetables and juices into a food processor and whizz to a chunky sauce.
2 Heat 2 more tablespoons of the oil in a large pan and fry the lamb over a high heat until browned. Lower the heat, stir in the tomato sauce and simmer, uncovered, for 20–30 minutes until the lamb is tender.
3 Cook the pasta according to the packet instructions. Drain and return to the pan with the pine nuts, herbs and remaining oil. Season and toss well before serving with the lamb.

• Per serving 864 kcalories, protein 46g, carbohydrate 72g, fat 46g, saturated fat 14g, fibre 3.2g, added sugar none, salt 0.69g

Vegetarians can use sliced mushrooms instead of the sausages in this unusual and healthy pasta dish.

Rigatoni with Sausage and Peas

300g/10oz rigatoni or penne
100g/4oz frozen peas
8 good-quality pork sausages,
such as Cumberland
1 tbsp olive oil
pinch of chilli flakes
grated zest of 1 lemon
1 tbsp wholegrain mustard
200g carton half-fat crème fraîche
handful of fresh basil leaves, torn

Takes 25 minutes • Serves 4

1 Cook the pasta in a large pan of salted boiling water for 8–10 minutes, or according to the packet instructions, until tender. Three minutes before the pasta is ready, tip in the peas and cook with the pasta.
2 While the pasta is cooking, split open the sausage skins and squeeze out the meat. Heat the oil in a frying pan and stir fry the meat for 3–4 minutes, until golden.
3 Add the chilli and lemon zest to the meat and cook for 1 minute. Stir in the mustard and crème fraîche and simmer for 1–2 minutes. Drain the pasta and peas and stir into the sausagemeat mixture. Season well, stir in the basil and serve.

• Per serving 665 kcalories, protein 28g, carbohydrate 68g, fat 33g, saturated fat 23g, fibre 4g, added sugar none, salt 2.43g

This dish tastes even better served with a chilled
Australian Chardonnay.

Italian Chicken with Tagliatelle

4 chicken breasts, preferably
part-boned
2 tbsp olive oil, plus extra
for greasing
4 pancetta or bacon rashers, halved
140g/5oz mushrooms, sliced
2 garlic cloves, crushed
2 tbsp chopped fresh parsley
350g/12oz tagliatelle
250g/9oz frozen baby broad beans
1 bunch of spring onions, trimmed
and chopped
4 tbsp whipping cream, or to taste

Takes 50 minutes • Serves 4

1 Preheat the oven to 190°C/Gas 5/fan oven
170°C and put the chicken in a single layer
in an oiled ovenproof dish. Heat the oil in a
frying pan and fry the pancetta or bacon until
crispy. Remove and set aside.
2 Add the mushrooms to the pan and fry
gently until they release their liquid, then
increase the heat and add the garlic and
seasoning. Cook until the moisture is driven
off, then stir in the parsley and spoon over
the chicken with the pancetta or bacon.
Roast in the oven for 20 minutes.
3 Meanwhile, cook the pasta according to
the packet instructions until tender, adding the
frozen beans for the last 3 minutes. Drain and
return to the pan with the onions and cream.
Season and toss together, adding more cream
if you like. Serve topped with the chicken.

• Per serving 665 kcalories, protein 53g, carbohydrate
73g, fat 20g, saturated fat 6.9g, fibre 7.5g, added
sugar none, salt 1.02g

Make the most of fresh spring ingredients for
a seasonal supper or lunch.

Smoked Salmon and Asparagus Pasta

25g/1oz butter
6 spring onions, trimmed and sliced
6 tbsp dry white wine or vermouth
200g carton crème fraîche
pinch of freshly grated nutmeg
2 tbsp chopped fresh dill (optional)
juice of ½ lemon
175g/6oz shelled broad beans
(700g/1lb 9oz in their pods)
350g/12oz spirali or spaghetti
175g/6oz young asparagus,
trimmed and halved
or cut into thirds
100g/4oz smoked salmon, cut into
small pieces

Takes 25 minutes • Serves 4

1 Melt the butter in a pan and fry the onions for 1 minute. Add the wine or vermouth and boil until reduced to about 2 tablespoons. Stir in the crème fraîche, nutmeg and seasoning. Bring to the boil and simmer for 2–3 minutes until slightly thickened. Stir in the dill, if using, and squeeze in a little lemon juice. Set aside.
2 Blanch the beans in salted boiling water for 2–3 minutes. Drain and refresh under running cold water. Drain again and peel off the skins.
3 Cook the pasta in salted boiling water according to the packet instructions, adding the asparagus 3 minutes before the end. Drain well, reserving a little pasta water. Toss the pasta and asparagus with the beans, smoked salmon and sauce, loosening with a spoonful or two of pasta water, if needed.

• Per serving 626 kcalories, protein 22g, carbohydrate 71g, fat 29g, saturated fat 16g, fibre 6g, added sugar none, salt 1.35g

A new twist on a classic recipe. For an even healthier version, use turkey mince, as it's brilliantly low in fat.

Spaghetti Bolognese

2 tbsp olive oil
1 onion, finely chopped
1 celery stick, finely chopped
450g/1lb lean minced beef
2 garlic cloves, crushed
2 tbsp sun-dried tomato purée
400g can chopped tomatoes
150ml/¼ pint beef stock
350g/12oz spaghetti
50g/2oz pitted black olives, chopped (optional)
handful of basil leaves, torn

Takes about 1 hour • Serves 4

1 Heat the oil in a large pan and fry the onion and celery gently for 5 minutes or until softened. Add the beef and garlic and fry for 3–4 minutes until the meat has browned, pressing with a spoon to remove any lumps. Stir in the tomato purée, then tip in the tomatoes. Swirl the stock in the tomato can, pour into the pan and bring to the boil. Season, cover and simmer gently for 35–40 minutes, stirring occasionally.
2 About 15 minutes before the end of cooking, boil the spaghetti according to the packet instructions until tender.
3 Stir the olives, if using, and basil into the sauce and heat through. Drain the spaghetti, toss with the sauce and serve straight away.

• Per serving 594 kcalories, protein 37g, carbohydrate 69g, fat 20g, saturated fat 5.7g, fibre 4g, added sugar none, salt 0.69g

Create an unusual supper for two using just
a few simple ingredients.

Stroganoff with Parsley Noodles

2 tbsp olive oil
1 onion, thinly sliced
2 steaks (fillet, sirloin or rump –
whatever you like best), cut into
bite-sized chunks
1 garlic clove, crushed
1 tsp paprika, plus extra for
sprinkling
1 tbsp tomato purée
300ml/½ pint beef stock
175g/6oz tagliatelle
knob of butter
handful of fresh flatleaf parsley,
chopped
142ml carton soured cream

Takes 30 minutes • Serves 2

1 Heat the oil in a deep frying pan and cook the onion gently for about 5 minutes until softened but not coloured. Tip in the steak and garlic, increase the heat and cook briskly until the meat is browned on all sides. Lower the heat and stir in the paprika, tomato purée and stock. Season, then simmer gently until the pasta is ready.
2 Cook the tagliatelle in a large pan of salted boiling water according to the packet instructions, until tender. Drain and return to the pan, then toss with the butter and parsley.
3 Stir all but 2 tablespoons of the soured cream into the stroganoff and heat through gently, then serve with the pasta, topped with the remaining soured cream and a sprinkling of paprika.

• Per serving 895 kcalories, protein 58g, carbohydrate 77g, fat 42g, saturated fat 17.1g, fibre 4g, added sugar none, salt 0.91g

Vegetarians can omit the chicken and stir in a 400g can of chickpeas (drained) 5 minutes before the end of the roasting time.

Mediterranean Chicken Pasta

2 boneless skinless chicken breasts, cut into chunks
1 red onion, cut into 8 wedges
1 red pepper, seeded and cut into 8 strips
2 garlic cloves, unpeeled
3 tbsp olive oil
300g/10oz short pasta shapes, such as rigatoni
4 tbsp pesto
200g/8oz cherry tomatoes, halved
100g/4oz firm goat's cheese or feta

Takes 35–45 minutes • Serves 4

1 Preheat the oven to 200°C/Gas 6/fan oven 180°C. Put the chicken, onion, red pepper and garlic cloves in a roasting tin and drizzle with the oil. Season. Mix with a spoon and roast for 20 minutes.
2 After the chicken has been cooking for 5 minutes, cook the pasta in a pan of salted boiling water according to the packet instructions. Drain well.
3 When the chicken and vegetables are cooked, remove from the oven. Slip the garlic out of its skin and mash in the tin with a spoon, then tip in the pasta, pesto and tomatoes and carefully mix together. Crumble the cheese over the top, check the seasoning and serve.

• Per serving 605 kcalories, protein 34g, carbohydrate 64g, fat 26g, saturated fat 9g, fibre 4g, added sugar none, salt 0.78g

A quick and tasty topping jazzes up a plain chicken breast and turns it into a classy supper dish.

Pesto Chicken with Fettuccine

2 boneless skinless chicken breasts
2 tbsp pesto
2 tbsp freshly grated parmesan cheese
2 tsp plain flour
175g/6oz fettuccine
2 tbsp extra virgin olive oil
1 red pepper, seeded and cut into thin strips

Takes 35 minutes • Serves 2

1 Preheat the oven to 200°C/Gas 6/fan oven 180°C. Slash each chicken breast on its smooth, rounded side with a sharp knife and spread with the pesto, working it into the slashes. Mix the parmesan and flour with plenty of coarsely ground black pepper, then press on to the pesto with your hands. Bake for 20 minutes until cooked through.
2 Meanwhile, cook the fettuccine in a large pan of salted boiling water for 8–10 minutes, or according to the packet instructions, until tender.
3 Drain the fettuccine and return to the pan. Add the olive oil and pepper strips and toss to combine. Slice the chicken, following the line of the slashes, and serve on top of the fettuccine.

• Per serving 670 kcalories, protein 52g, carbohydrate 74g, fat 21g, saturated fat 5.4g, fibre 2.9g, added sugar none, salt 0.6g

Bring the flavours of sunny Spain into your home with this flavoursome dish.

Tagliatelle Paella

3 tbsp olive oil
3 boneless skinless chicken breasts, cut into small chunks
1 medium onion, finely chopped
2 garlic cloves, crushed
2 bay leaves
2 red peppers, seeded and sliced
175g/6oz fresh or frozen peas
175g/6oz fresh or frozen broad beans
150ml/¼ pint white wine
650g/1lb 7oz fresh mussels
400g/14oz tagliatelle
425ml/¾ pint chicken stock
large pinch of saffron threads, infused in 2 tbsp boiling water
450g/1lb large peeled raw prawns
284ml carton double cream
large handful of fresh parsley, chopped

Takes about 1 hour • Serves 6

1 Heat the oil in a large, wide pan and cook the chicken for 4–5 minutes. Add the onion, garlic, bay leaves and peppers and cook for 4–5 minutes. Add the peas and beans and fry for 2–3 minutes. Remove from the heat.
2 Bring the wine to a simmer in a large saucepan. Tip in the mussels, cover and cook for 3–5 minutes until they open. Drain over a bowl to catch the juices, discarding any that are closed.
3 Cook the tagliatelle according to the packet instructions. Meanwhile, pour the stock, mussel liquid and saffron over the chicken and vegetables, bring to a simmer, then add the prawns and cream and cook for 3–4 minutes. Toss in the mussels, parsley and seasoning and heat through. Drain the tagliatelle, stir into the sauce and serve.

• Per serving 724 kcalories, protein 49g, carbohydrate 57g, fat 33g, saturated fat 16g, fibre 6g, added sugar none, salt 3.54g

The arrival of new season English asparagus in May is the perfect excuse for cooking this impressive, creamy dish.

Farfalle with Chicken and Asparagus

500g/1lb 2oz asparagus, trimmed
2 lemons
100g/4oz thinly sliced pancetta or rindless streaky bacon
500g/1lb 2oz farfalle (pasta bows)
50g/2oz butter
284ml carton double cream
2 cooked boneless skinless chicken breasts, torn into strips
50g/2oz parmesan cheese, freshly grated
few gratings of fresh nutmeg

Takes 35 minutes • Serves 4–6

1 Cut the asparagus into short lengths on the diagonal, keeping the tips separate. Cook the stems in salted boiling water for 4 minutes, add the tips and cook for 1 minute more. Drain and refresh under cold running water.
2 Peel and segment the lemons, removing the pith, then cut the segments into small pieces and put them in a bowl with any juice. Grill the pancetta or bacon for 3–4 minutes until crisp.
3 Cook the pasta in salted boiling water until tender. Meanwhile, simmer the butter and half the cream in a large pan for 2–3 minutes until slightly thickened. Tip in the lemons and juice, chicken and asparagus. Turn off the heat.
4 Drain the pasta and add to the chicken with the rest of the cream. Toss well, adding the parmesan and nutmeg. Season and serve topped with the pancetta or bacon.

• Per serving for four 1122 kcalories, protein 47g, carbohydrate 100g, fat 63g, saturated fat 33.4g, fibre 6g, added sugar none, salt 1.89g

As soon as you cut into the egg, the yolk runs through the pasta, creating a rich sauce.

Linguine with Asparagus and Egg

450g/1lb asparagus
350g/12oz fresh linguine or
fine tagliatelle
1 tbsp light olive oil
4 medium eggs
2 tbsp walnut oil
50g/2oz vegetarian parmesan
cheese, freshly grated

Takes 30–35 minutes • Serves 4

1 Snap the woody ends off the asparagus and discard. Cut the stems in half widthways, then cook in simmering salted water until just tender, 3–4 minutes. Drain and refresh under cold running water, then drain again.

2 Cook the pasta according to the packet instructions, until tender. Heat the olive oil in a frying pan over a low heat and gently break in the eggs. Cover and cook for 3–4 minutes until the whites have set and the yolks are still runny.

3 In the meantime, drain the pasta and toss it back in the pan with the asparagus and walnut oil. Divide between four warmed bowls, top with the eggs and scatter with sea salt and the parmesan.

• Per serving 365 kcalories, protein 18g, carbohydrate 41g, fat 16g, saturated fat 3g, fibre 4g, added sugar none, salt 0.19g

A seasonal celebration of fresh summer vegetables that makes the perfect weekend lunch.

Pasta Primavera

85g/3oz unsalted butter
1½ tbsp each chopped fresh parsley,
mint and chives
400g/14oz tagliatelle
200g/8oz baby carrots, preferably
with a little stalk left on
400g/14oz shelled garden peas,
about 1.25kg/2lb 12oz
in their pods
200g/8oz fine green beans, trimmed
200g/8oz baby or regular-sized
courgettes, thickly sliced
splash of olive oil
finely grated zest and juice
of 1 lemon
as many fresh basil leaves
as you like

Takes 30 minutes • Serves 4

1 Gently melt the butter with the herbs. Set aside. Bring two large pans of salted water to the boil (one for the pasta, the other for the vegetables). Tip the pasta into one pan and cook according to the packet instructions.
2 While the pasta cooks, cook the carrots in the other pan for 2 minutes. Add the peas, beans and courgettes and cook for 3 minutes more.
3 Drain both pasta and vegetables well. Return the pasta to its pan and toss with the oil, half the herb butter and the lemon zest and juice. Return the vegetables to their pan, toss with the rest of the butter and seasoning. Spoon the pasta into bowls, grind black pepper over and top with the vegetables and basil.

• Per serving 634 kcalories, protein 21g, carbohydrate 93g, fat 22g, saturated fat 12g, fibre 11g, added sugar none, salt 0.09g

If you have any of this delicious pesto left over, try it on top
of grilled or barbecued lamb chops.

Spaghetti with Pea and Mint Pesto

250g/9oz shelled fresh peas, just
under 900g/2lb in their pods
2 fat garlic cloves, finely chopped
50g/2oz pine nuts, toasted
50g/2oz parmesan cheese, chopped
into small chunks
good handful of fresh mint leaves
(about 20g/¾oz)
6 tbsp extra virgin olive oil
350g/12oz spaghetti

TO SERVE
freshly grated vegetarian
parmesan cheese
extra virgin olive oil

Takes 35–40 minutes • Serves 4

1 Cook the peas in boiling water for
2–3 minutes until just tender, then drain
and refresh under cold running water. Pat
dry, then tip into a food processor and add
the garlic, pine nuts, parmesan, mint and oil.
Season, then pulse very briefly until the
ingredients are roughly chopped.
2 Cook the spaghetti according to the packet
instructions until tender. Drain, reserving some
of the water, then toss with the pesto and
about 2 tablespoons of the water.
3 Pile into warmed bowls and serve at once,
with parmesan and olive oil at the table.

• Per serving 640 kcalories, protein 21g, carbohydrate
72g, fat 32g, saturated fat 6g, fibre 6g, added sugar
none, salt 0.30g

You can make the mozzarella butter in advance and freeze it, so that you'll always be ready to whip up this delicious and unusual pasta dish.

Pumpkin Pasta

3 tbsp olive oil
2 garlic cloves, crushed
125g ball mozzarella cheese, roughly chopped
50g/2oz unsalted butter, softened
small handful of fresh sage leaves, plus extra to serve
grated zest and juice of 1 lemon
500g/1lb 2oz piece of pumpkin (unpeeled weight), peeled, seeded and cut into 2cm/¾in cubes
300g/10oz conchiglie (pasta shells)
85g/3oz vegetarian parmesan cheese, freshly grated

Takes about 1 hour • Serves 4

1 Heat 1 tablespoon of the oil in a small pan and soften the garlic, then blend to a coarse paste in a food processor with the mozzarella, butter, sage, lemon zest and juice and seasoning. Transfer to a piece of parchment paper or cling film, roll into a cylinder and chill for at least 30 minutes.
2 Preheat the oven to 200°C/Gas 6/fan oven 180°C. Heat the remaining oil in a roasting tin in the oven for 5 minutes. Toss in the pumpkin, season and roast for 25–30 minutes, turning occasionally.
3 Cook the pasta according to the packet instructions. Drain and return to the pan with the pumpkin and parmesan. Slice the butter, add to the pan and toss to mix and melt. Serve topped with sage.

• Per serving 634 kcalories, protein 26g, carbohydrate 60g, fat 34g, saturated fat 17g, fibre 4g, added sugar none, salt 1.10g

Cooking the broccoli with the pasta adds flavour to the finished dish.

Spaghetti with Broccoli and Tomatoes

400g/14oz spaghetti
300g/10oz broccoli, trimmed and cut into small florets
3 tbsp olive oil
1 onion, finely chopped
2 garlic cloves, crushed
1 fresh red chilli, seeded and finely chopped
2 sun-blush or sun-dried tomatoes, snipped into small pieces
4 ripe plum tomatoes, roughly chopped
freshly grated vegetarian parmesan cheese, to serve

Takes 30 minutes • Serves 4

1 Coil the spaghetti into a large pan of salted boiling water, bring back to the boil and cook for 8 minutes. Add the broccoli florets and continue boiling for another 3–4 minutes or until the spaghetti is tender.
2 While the pasta is cooking, heat the oil in a separate pan and gently cook the onion, garlic and chilli for about 5 minutes until softened but not browned. Tip in both types of tomatoes, season and simmer for a further 5 minutes.
3 Drain the pasta and broccoli, reserving some of the water. Toss with the tomato mixture, moistening with water if necessary. Spoon into four warmed bowls and serve with parmesan.

• Per serving 474 kcalories, protein 17g, carbohydrate 82g, fat 11g, saturated fat 1.5g, fibre 6.4g, added sugar none, salt 0.11g

Meat eaters can tip in some crispy bacon as well. Alternatively, use asparagus or green beans instead of the broad beans.

Pasta with Broad Beans

500g/1lb 2oz short pasta shapes, such as rigatoni or penne
6 tbsp extra virgin olive oil, plus extra for sprinkling
2 garlic cloves, finely chopped
½ tsp chilli flakes
500g/1lb 2oz fresh or frozen broad beans, thawed if frozen
2 tbsp finely chopped fresh parsley
1 tbsp freshly grated vegetarian parmesan cheese, plus extra to serve

Takes 30 minutes • Serves 4

1 Cook the pasta in a large pan of salted boiling water until tender.
2 At the same time, heat the oil in a large frying pan. Fry the garlic and chilli flakes over a medium to high heat for 1 minute. Add the broad beans with 3 tablespoons water and cook for 3–5 minutes until the beans are tender and the water has evaporated.
3 Drain the pasta and tip into the broad beans with the parsley and parmesan. Toss well and season. Serve sprinkled with olive oil and grated parmesan.

• Per serving 713 kcalories, protein 25g, carbohydrate 104g, fat 25g, saturated fat 4g, fibre 12g, added sugar none, salt 0.2g

A quick and easy supper idea that children will love
as much as adults.

Cheesy Corn and Broccoli Pasta

100g/4oz farfalle (pasta bows)
140g/5oz broccoli florets
198g can sweetcorn, drained
and rinsed
25g/1oz butter
100ml/3½fl oz milk
100g/4oz cheddar cheese, grated

Takes 15 minutes • Serves 2

1 Cook the pasta in a large pan of salted boiling water for 8–10 minutes, or according to the packet instructions, until tender. Add the broccoli and sweetcorn to the water for the last 4 minutes.
2 While the pasta is cooking, melt the butter in a medium saucepan with the milk, then bring to the boil and remove from the heat. Tip in the cheese and stir until melted.
3 Drain the pasta and vegetables well, return to the pan and pour in the sauce. Toss to mix and season to taste before serving.

• Per serving 620 kcalories, protein 26g, carbohydrate 63g, fat 31g, saturated fat 18.2g, fibre 4.5g, added sugar 6g, salt 1.75g

Try using feta, stilton, goat's cheese or even cheddar
instead of the brie.

Summer Pasta with Melting Brie

300g/10oz short pasta shapes
250g/9oz green beans, trimmed
250g/9oz ripe tomatoes
200g/8oz ripe brie cheese
1 garlic clove, chopped
juice of ½ lemon
3 tbsp good olive oil

Takes 25 minutes • Serves 4

1 Cook the pasta in a large pan of salted boiling water according to the packet instructions. Halfway through the cooking time (after about 5 minutes), throw in the green beans.

2 While the pasta and beans are cooking, chop the tomatoes and brie quite small and mix with the garlic, lemon juice and olive oil. Season with salt and freshly ground black pepper.

3 Drain the pasta and return it to the pan. Add the tomato and brie mixture and mix everything over a low heat until the brie starts to melt. Serve straight away.

• Per serving 522 kcalories, protein 20g, carbohydrate 61g, fat 24g, saturated fat 10g, fibre 4g, added sugar none, salt 0.92g

Mushrooms add a deliciously nutty flavour and juicy texture to this veggie-friendly pasta.

Tagliatelle with Goat's Cheese

250g/9oz chestnut mushrooms
1 small onion
2 garlic cloves
175g/6oz tagliatelle
25g/1oz butter
1 tbsp olive oil, plus extra for drizzling
100g/4oz firm goat's cheese
freshly shaved vegetarian parmesan cheese, to serve

Takes 20 minutes • Serves 2 (easily doubled)

1 Slice the mushrooms and finely chop the onion and garlic. Cook the pasta in plenty of salted boiling water according to the packet instructions.
2 Heat the butter and oil in a frying pan until the butter has melted. Add the onion and cook until golden, about 3–4 minutes. Stir in the garlic and mushrooms and cook, stirring, until the mushrooms are golden brown.
3 Drain the pasta, reserving 4 tablespoons of the water. Return the pasta to its pan with the water and stir in the mushroom mixture. Roughly break the goat's cheese into pieces and gently stir it into the pasta so it starts to melt. Serve sprinkled with black pepper, a drizzle of olive oil and a few shavings of parmesan.

• Per serving 598 kcalories, protein 20g, carbohydrate 71g, fat 28g, saturated fat 8g, fibre 5g, added sugar none, salt 0.88g

This vegetarian version of the classic bolognese sauce is cheap to make and superhealthy too – it's particularly high in iron.

Veggie Bolognese

1 onion
1 carrot
1 celery stick
1 red pepper, cored and seeded
2 tbsp olive oil
100g/4oz red lentils
400g can tomatoes
600ml/1 pint vegetable stock
2 tsp dried oregano
½ tsp ground cinnamon
350g/12oz spaghetti
freshly grated vegetarian parmesan cheese, to serve

Takes 35–45 minutes • Serves 4

1 Roughly chop the vegetables, then whizz in a food processor until finely chopped.
2 Heat the oil in a large saucepan and fry the vegetables for about 8 minutes until soft. Stir in the lentils, tomatoes, stock, oregano and cinnamon. Bring to the boil and season to taste, then reduce the heat, cover and simmer for 20 minutes.
3 Cook the spaghetti in a large pan of salted boiling water for 10–12 minutes, or according to the packet instructions, until tender. Drain well and serve with the sauce and grated cheese.

• Per serving 484 kcalories, protein 19g, carbohydrate 90g, fat 8g, saturated fat 1g, fibre 6g, added sugar none, salt 0.66g

Roasting the squash brings out its sweet nutty flavour
and the onions add a savoury note.

Rigatoni with Roasted Squash

1 butternut squash, about
700g/1lb 9oz
2 red onions
2 garlic cloves, sliced
2 tbsp olive oil
175g/6oz rigatoni or penne
3 rounded tbsp crème fraîche
freshly grated vegetarian parmesan
cheese, to serve (optional)

Takes 50 minutes • Serves 2 generously

1 Preheat the oven to 200°C/Gas 6/fan oven 180°C. Peel, halve and seed the squash, then cut into bite-sized chunks and tip into a roasting tin. Peel the onions, leaving the roots intact, then cut each one lengthways into 8 wedges and add them to the tin with the garlic, oil and seasoning. Toss until all the ingredients are glistening, then roast for 30 minutes.
2 Meanwhile, cook the pasta in salted boiling water for 8–10 minutes, or according to the packet instructions, until tender. Drain, reserving 4 tablespoons of the water.
3 Remove the tin from the oven and stir in the 4 tablespoons water and the crème fraîche, then toss in the pasta. Serve sprinkled with black pepper and parmesan if you like.

• Per serving 572 kcalories, protein 16.7g, carbohydrate 102g, fat 13.8g, saturated fat 7.6g, fibre 9.2g, added sugar none, salt 0.16g

Good-quality wheat-free pasta using alternative grains and cereals is now available from larger supermarkets.

Pasta and Peppers with Walnut Pesto

FOR THE PESTO
25g/1oz walnut pieces
2 garlic cloves, crushed
grated zest of 1 large lemon
20g pack fresh parsley
4 tbsp extra virgin olive oil

FOR THE PASTA
2 small red onions, quartered and separated into pieces
1 tbsp extra virgin olive oil
250g pack wheat-free pasta (rice and corn is good)
290g jar mixed pepper antipasto, drained and sliced
50g/2oz vegetarian parmesan cheese, freshly grated, plus extra shavings to serve

Takes 35 minutes • Serves 3

1 Make the pesto. Finely chop the walnuts, garlic and lemon zest in a food processor. Add the parsley and oil, season, then whizz again to combine.
2 Preheat the grill to high. Toss the onions with 1 tablespoon oil in the grill pan, spread out in a single layer and grill for 6–8 minutes until slightly charred.
3 Meanwhile, cook the pasta according to the packet instructions until just tender – it doesn't swell as much as wheat pasta, so taste a piece to check it's tender. Drain.
4 Tip the pesto, onions and peppers into the pasta pan and put back on the heat. Stir for a few moments, then toss in the pasta and cheese. Season and serve scattered with cheese shavings.

• Per serving 696 kcalories, protein 17g, carbohydrate 74g, fat 40g, saturated fat 8g, fibre 5g, added sugar none, salt 2.74g

Tossing the spinach into the hot ingredients just before serving preserves both its vitamins and texture.

Roasted Vegetable and Feta Pasta

1 small butternut squash, peeled, seeded and cut into chunks
1 large red pepper, seeded and cut into chunks
2 garlic cloves, roughly chopped
60g/2½oz feta cheese, crumbled
1 tsp finely chopped fresh rosemary
1 tbsp olive oil
200g/8oz penne or other short pasta shapes
100g/4oz baby spinach leaves

Takes 45–55 minutes • Serves 2

1 Preheat the oven to 200°C/Gas 6/fan oven 180°C. Put the squash, pepper, garlic, feta and rosemary into a large roasting tin. Sprinkle over the oil and plenty of black pepper. Toss until lightly coated, then roast for 30–40 minutes, tossing after 15 minutes.
2 Meanwhile, cook the pasta in a large pan of salted boiling water for 8 minutes, or according to the packet instructions, until tender.
3 Take the tin from the oven. Scoop out about half a mugful of the pasta water. Drain the pasta and toss it into the tin with the spinach. Stir until the spinach starts to wilt, adding a splash of the reserved water to moisten if necessary. Serve straight away.

• Per serving 605 kcalories, protein 22g, carbohydrate 104g, fat 14g, saturated fat 5g, fibre 10g, added sugar none, salt 1.34g

This simple and delicious supper dish for two combines larder ingredients in a slightly unusual way. Serve with a green salad.

Veggie Pasta with Goat's Cheese

200g/8oz farfalle (pasta bows)
100g/4oz frozen peas
finely grated zest of 1 lemon
2 tbsp extra virgin olive oil
100g/4oz goat's cheese, crumbled
100g/4oz chargrilled (antipasto)
peppers from a jar,
torn into strips

Takes 25 minutes • Serves 2

1 Tip the pasta into a large pan of salted boiling water, give it a good stir and cook on a rolling boil for the time stated on the packet, stirring once or twice. Three minutes before the pasta is ready, throw in the peas.
2 When the pasta and peas are cooked, drain, saving some of the water, then tip the pasta and peas back into the pan. Over a low heat, stir in the lemon zest and 1 tablespoon of the oil, then stir in 4 tablespoons of the pasta water, the goat's cheese and pepper strips.
3 Season and heat through until the cheese begins to melt. Spoon the pasta and peas into warmed bowls and sprinkle with black pepper and the remaining oil. Serve straight away.

• Per serving 671 kcalories, protein 22g, carbohydrate 85g, fat 29g, saturated fat 3g, fibre 7g, added sugar none, salt 2.5g

Pasta dishes don't come much easier than this! Only six ingredients, hardly any chopping and an Italian feast ready in under an hour.

Fusilli with Roasted Vegetables

1 medium red onion, cut into wedges
2 courgettes, cut into chunks
3 garlic cloves, unpeeled
3 tbsp olive oil
250g pack cherry tomatoes
140g/5oz fusilli or other short pasta shapes
handful of basil leaves
freshly grated vegetarian parmesan cheese, to serve

Takes 45–55 minutes • Serves 2

1 Preheat the oven to 220°C/Gas 7/fan oven 200°C. Put the onion, courgettes and garlic into a large ovenproof dish. Add the oil, season well and stir, then roast for 15 minutes. Stir in the tomatoes and continue roasting for 15 minutes more.
2 Meanwhile, cook the pasta in salted boiling water for 8–10 minutes, or according to the packet instructions, until tender.
3 Drain the pasta. Take the vegetables out of the oven and pop the garlic cloves out of their skins. Mash the garlic against the side of the dish and stir through the vegetables. Tip in the pasta and toss everything together, tearing in some basil as you go. Serve with parmesan.

• Per serving 460 kcalories, protein 12g, carbohydrate 64g, fat 19g, saturated fat 3g, fibre 5g, added sugar none, salt 0.07g

A creamy, all-in-one sauce that smells delicious –
this is comfort food at its best.

Cheesy Leek and Spinach Pasta

good knob of butter
1 tbsp olive oil
2 large leeks, total weight about
450g/1lb, thinly sliced
500g pack penne rigate or your
favourite pasta shape
200g carton crème fraîche
1 tbsp wholegrain mustard
125g pack Danish blue cheese,
roughly diced
8 sun-dried tomatoes in oil,
drained and thinly sliced
225g bag baby spinach leaves

Takes 25–35 minutes • Serves 4

1 Melt the butter with the oil in a large pan, tip in the leeks and splash in a little hot water. Cover and cook over a low heat, stirring occasionally, for about 10 minutes until no longer squeaky,
2 While the leeks are cooking, cook the pasta in salted boiling water according to the packet instructions. Meanwhile, tip the crème fraîche and mustard into the leeks, add three quarters of the cheese and season well. Stir until the cheese melts. Take off the heat.
3 Drain the pasta, reserving the water. Stir the pasta into the sauce, adding enough cooking water to make the sauce coat the pasta, and add the tomatoes. Stir in the spinach, a handful at a time, until it wilts, splashing in a little more water if needed. Toss in the remaining cheese and serve.

• Per serving 808 kcalories, protein 27g, carbohydrate 103g, fat 35g, saturated fat 18g, fibre 9g, added sugar none, salt 2.03g

An unusual alternative to the classic Italian pesto.
If you don't like broccoli, try making it with frozen peas.

Broccoli Pesto Pasta

400g/14oz rigatoni or other short
pasta shapes
250g/9oz broccoli florets
1 garlic clove, grated
finely grated zest of 1 lemon
½ tsp chilli flakes
3 tbsp pine nuts
juice of ½ lemon
5 tbsp extra virgin olive oil
3 tbsp freshly grated vegetarian
parmesan cheese

Takes 20 minutes • Serves 4

1 Cook the pasta according to the packet instructions until tender. Meanwhile, cook the broccoli in salted boiling water for 4 minutes, then drain and return to the pan. Mash the broccoli lightly, add the garlic, lemon zest, chilli flakes and pine nuts and toss to mix.
2 Drain the pasta and return it to the pan. Stir in the broccoli pesto, lemon juice and oil, then add seasoning and toss in the parmesan. Serve straight away.

• Per serving 604 kcalories, protein 19g, carbohydrate 79g, fat 26g, saturated fat 4g, fibre 5g, added sugar none, salt 0.47g

You can bump up the tomato taste by tossing in a few snipped
sun-blush or sun-dried tomatoes.

Tricolore Tagliatelle

400g/14oz tagliatelle
6 ripe tomatoes, finely chopped
100g bag rocket, roughly chopped
½ small red onion, finely chopped
2 tbsp capers, rinsed
4 tbsp extra virgin olive oil
250g carton ricotta cheese

Takes 15–20 minutes • Serves 4

1 Cook the tagliatelle in a large pan of salted boiling water for 8–10 minutes, or according to the packet instructions, until tender.
2 Meanwhile, mix together the tomatoes, rocket, onion and capers.
3 Drain the pasta and return it to the pan, off the heat. Pour in the oil and toss until the pasta glistens, then tip in the tomato mixture and toss again. Season well, add the ricotta in small spoonfuls and gently toss through. Serve in a large bowl.

• Per serving 587 kcalories, protein 20g, carbohydrate 81g, fat 23g, saturated fat 7g, fibre 5g, added sugar none, salt 0.58g

This is a lighter version of the traditional dish. Try adding other appropriate ingredients from your storecupboard.

Macaroni Cheese with Mushrooms

200g/8oz macaroni
2 tbsp olive oil
2 leeks, sliced
6 mushrooms, quartered
4 tomatoes, roughly chopped
100g/4oz garlic and herb soft cheese

Takes 20 minutes • Serves 2

1 Cook the macaroni in a large pan of salted boiling water for 8–10 minutes, or according to the packet instructions, until tender.
2 Meanwhile, heat the oil in a wok or deep frying pan and cook the leeks and mushrooms for 4–6 minutes or until the leeks are tender. Toss in the tomatoes, season well and cook for another minute.
3 Drain the macaroni, tip into the leek mixture and toss well to mix. Crumble the cheese on top and serve as soon as it starts to melt.

• Per serving 664 kcalories, protein 20g, carbohydrate 85g, fat 30g, saturated fat 11.7g, fibre 7.9g, added sugar none, salt 0.5g

These tiny tomatoes taste extra sweet when roasted,
and are a contrast to the salty cheese.

Spaghetti with Feta and Tomatoes

500g/1lb 2oz cherry tomatoes
3 tbsp olive oil
400g/14oz spaghetti
250g/9oz Greek feta cheese
generous handful of fresh flatleaf
parsley (or a supermarket pack)
handful of olives
freshly grated vegetarian parmesan
cheese, to serve

Takes 25 minutes • Serves 4

1 Preheat the oven to 200°C/Gas 6/fan oven 180°C. Tip the tomatoes into a shallow ovenproof dish, drizzle over the olive oil and season. Roast for 15 minutes until slightly scorched.

2 Cook the spaghetti in plenty of salted boiling water for 10–12 minutes, until just tender. Meanwhile, cut the feta into cubes and roughly chop the parsley.

3 Drain the pasta, then return to the pan. Add the roasted tomatoes, along with their pan juices, the feta, olives and parsley. Toss together until well mixed, then serve with freshly grated parmesan for sprinkling.

• Per serving 530 kcalories, protein 23g, carbohydrate 79g, fat 16g, saturated fat 8g, fibre 5g, added sugar none, salt 3.02g

Enjoy the rich flavours of Italy in this easy, all-in-one tomato and basil lasagne – perfect for relaxed entertaining on a summer evening.

Two-cheese Lasagne with Pesto

250g pack fresh lasagne sheets

FOR THE SAUCE
1.2 litres/2 pints milk
100g/4oz butter
100g/4oz plain flour
pinch of freshly grated nutmeg

FOR THE FILLING
500g/1lb 2oz baby spinach leaves
3 rounded tbsp good-quality pesto
500g/1lb 2oz cherry tomatoes
on the vine
good handful of basil leaves
175g/6oz parmesan cheese,
freshly grated
2 × 125–150g balls mozzarella
cheese (preferably buffalo),
torn into pieces

Takes about 1½ hours • Serves 6

1 Preheat the oven to 200°C/Gas 6/fan oven 180°C. Put all the sauce ingredients in a pan and simmer, whisking, until thick and smooth. Season and cool.
2 Pour a kettleful of boiling water over the spinach in a large bowl. Leave for 30 seconds, then drain. Rinse, drain and squeeze dry.
3 Spread 1–2 spoonfuls of sauce over the base of an ovenproof dish (30 × 20 × 6cm/ 12 × 8 × 2½in). Lay a third of the lasagne on top and spread with a third of the sauce, then swirl a spoonful of pesto through with a knife. Scatter over half the spinach, then a third of the tomatoes, some basil and a third of the cheeses. Season. Repeat these layers, then finish with a layer of lasagne, sauce, pesto, tomatoes and cheeses. Season and bake for 35–40 minutes. Serve scattered with basil.

• Per serving 711 kcalories, protein 38g, carbohydrate 46g, fat 43g, saturated fat 25g, fibre 4g, added sugar none, salt 2.5g

You can prepare this dish several hours ahead, so it's ideal for when you're having friends round for supper.

Rigatoni Sausage Bake

1 tbsp olive oil
1 onion, chopped
400g/14oz good-quality pork
sausages, skins discarded
and meat chopped
1 large carrot, grated
150ml/¼ pint red wine
300ml/½ pint vegetable stock
3 tbsp tomato purée
500g pack rigatoni
200g/8oz fresh spinach
140g/5oz mature cheddar
cheese, grated

FOR THE WHITE SAUCE
50g/2oz butter
50g/2oz plain flour
600ml/1 pint milk
good pinch of freshly grated nutmeg

Takes about 1¼ hours • Serves 6

1 Preheat the oven to 190°C/Gas 5/fan oven 170°C. Heat the oil in a large pan and fry the onion for 5 minutes until softened. Stir in the sausagemeat and fry until lightly coloured. Add the carrot, wine, stock, purée and seasoning. Bring to the boil and simmer uncovered for 15 minutes until thickened.
2 Put all the sauce ingredients in a pan with some seasoning and simmer, whisking all the time, until thick and smooth.
3 Cook the pasta according to the packet instructions, remove from the heat and stir in the spinach until just wilted, then drain. Spread half the pasta and spinach in a shallow 2.2-litre/4-pint ovenproof dish. Cover with the sausage sauce, then the remaining pasta and the white sauce. Sprinkle with the cheese and bake for 25 minutes until golden brown.

• Per serving 749 kcalories, protein 31g, carbohydrate 84g, fat 33g, saturated fat 16g, fibre 5g, added sugar none, salt 2.32g

Serve this impressive pasta bake with a mixed salad and crusty bread.

Goat's Cheese and Mushroom Pasta Shells

20g sachet dried porcini mushrooms, soaked in 150ml/¼ pint hot water for 20 minutes
50g/2oz butter
2 shallots or 1 small onion, finely chopped
200g/8oz chestnut mushrooms, sliced
1 garlic clove, chopped
3 tbsp chopped fresh parsley
200g/8oz large pasta shells (conchiglione)
500g/1lb 2oz cherry tomatoes, halved
2 tbsp olive oil, plus a little extra
200g/8oz firm goat's cheese, chopped
50g/2oz parmesan cheese, freshly grated

Takes about 1½ hours • Serves 4

1 Drain the porcini in a sieve lined with kitchen paper. Reserve the liquid. Melt the butter in a large pan and fry the shallots or onion gently for 5 minutes. Add the chestnut mushrooms and fry until softened, then add the porcini, garlic, soaking liquid and seasoning. Cook uncovered until almost dry, stir in the parsley and remove from the heat.

2 Preheat the oven to 190°C/Gas 5/fan oven 170°C. Boil the shells according to the packet instructions, drain and toss in a little oil.

3 Stand the tomatoes in a shallow 1.4-litre/2½-pint ovenproof dish and sprinkle with oil and seasoning. Stuff the shells with the mushrooms, place on top of the tomatoes and push in the goat's cheese. Cover and bake for 20 minutes, then uncover, sprinkle with parmesan and bake for a further 20 minutes.

• Per serving 578 kcalories, protein 24g, carbohydrate 46g, fat 34g, saturated fat 19g, fibre 4g, added sugar none, salt 1.54g

A light and simple summer supper dish.
It's delicious served with a crisp green salad.

Swiss Tagliatelle Bake

olive oil, for brushing
400g/14oz tagliatelle
25g/1oz butter
100g/4oz white button
mushrooms, sliced
142ml carton whipping or
double cream
100g/4oz ham, cut into
chunky strips
85g/3oz gruyère or
emmental cheese
250g pack cherry tomatoes, halved
50g/2oz parmesan cheese

Takes 40 minutes • Serves 4

1 Preheat the oven to 190°C/Gas 5/fan oven 170°C and brush the inside of a shallow 1.2-litre/2-pint ovenproof dish with oil. Cook the tagliatelle in a large pan of salted boiling water according to the packet instructions, until tender.
2 Meanwhile, melt the butter in a deep frying pan and cook the mushrooms gently for 5 minutes, stirring occasionally. Pour in the cream and bring to the boil, stirring, then remove from the heat and add the ham and about two thirds of the gruyère or emmental. Season and mix well.
3 Drain the pasta and mix with the sauce. Spread the mixture out in the dish and top with the tomatoes, cut-side up. Sprinkle with the remaining gruyère or emmental and the parmesan and bake for 20 minutes.

• Per serving 723 kcalories, protein 29g, carbohydrate 79g, fat 34g, saturated fat 19.7g, fibre 4g, added sugar none, salt 1.44g

In this new twist on a family favourite, the white sauce is replaced with crème fraîche, giving it a luxurious creamy touch.

Cauli-macaroni Cheese

300g/10oz rigatoni or penne
1 small cauliflower, cut into florets
200g carton crème fraîche
2 tsp wholegrain mustard
175g/6oz red leicester cheese, grated
2 tomatoes, cut into wedges

Takes 30 minutes • Serves 4

1 Bring a large pan of salted water to the boil. Toss in the pasta and bring back to the boil, then cook for a couple of minutes. Tip in the cauliflower and cook for a further 8–10 minutes until both are tender.

2 Drain the pasta and cauliflower well. Put the crème fraîche, mustard and most of the cheese into the pasta pan. Stir over a low heat just until the cheese starts to melt.

3 Preheat the grill to hot. Tip the pasta and cauliflower into the sauce and gently stir together. Season. Transfer to a flameproof dish, scatter the tomatoes on top, then the rest of the cheese and a sprinkling of black pepper. Grill for 5 minutes until brown and bubbling.

• Per serving 636 kcalories, protein 25g, carbohydrate 64g, fat 33g, saturated fat 18g, fibre 5g, added sugar none, salt 0.98g

This is a rich and luscious pasta bake,
so a little goes a long way.

Creamy Fish Lasagne

250g carton mascarpone cheese
250g carton ricotta cheese
284ml carton single cream
3 tbsp chopped fresh dill
2 tbsp lemon juice
300g/10oz broccoli, cut into
small florets
250g/9oz fresh lasagne sheets
450g/1lb salmon fillet, skinned and
cut into small chunks
3 rounded tbsp freshly grated
parmesan cheese

Takes 1–1¼ hours • Serves 4

1 Preheat the oven to 180°C/Gas 4/fan oven 160°C. Beat together the mascarpone, ricotta, cream, dill, lemon juice and seasoning.
2 Cook the broccoli in salted boiling water for 3 minutes, then drain and cool under running cold water. Drain well again.
3 Spread a little cream mixture over the base of an oiled shallow rectangular dish, about 25cm/10in long. Cover with a layer of lasagne, cutting it to fit and not overlapping the pieces. Spread with more cream mixture, then sprinkle over a third of the salmon and broccoli. Repeat twice more, then finish with lasagne and the remaining sauce. Sprinkle with parmesan and bake for 35–40 minutes until deep golden.

• Per serving 914 kcalories, protein 45g, carbohydrate 36g, fat 66g, saturated fat 35g, fibre 4g, added sugar none, salt 0.77g

An easy supper for two – just layer the pasta and sauce, and bake.
Serve with garlic bread, a mixed salad and a glass of wine.

Gooey Pasta Bake

500g carton Neapolitan pasta sauce
(from the chiller cabinet)
good handful of fresh basil leaves
250g pack fresh stuffed spinach and
ricotta tortellini
100g pack mozzarella cheese, sliced
2 tbsp freshly grated parmesan
cheese
1 tbsp pine nuts

Takes 40–55 minutes •
Serves 2 generously

1 Preheat the oven to 180°C/Gas 4/fan oven 160°C. Tip the pasta sauce into a large bowl and thin it down with 100ml/3½fl oz water. Scatter in the basil leaves and tortellini, season and give it all a really good stir.
2 Divide half of the pasta mixture between two gratin dishes and tear half of the mozzarella over them. Spoon the rest of the pasta mixture on top, press the pasta down into the sauce, then tear the remaining mozzarella over the sauce and scatter with the parmesan and pine nuts.
3 Put the dishes on a baking sheet to catch any spills and bake for 25–30 minutes until golden and bubbling.

• Per serving 735 kcalories, protein 30g, carbohydrate 22g, fat 59g, saturated fat 26g, fibre 2g, added sugar none, salt 4.84g

A couple of handfuls of crushed crisps will give the topping extra crunch. Use whatever cheese you have to hand.

Cheeseboard Pasta Bake

500g pack rigatoni or penne
850ml/1½ pints milk
50g/2oz butter
50g/2oz plain flour
½ nutmeg (or ¼ tsp ready ground)
200g/8oz cooked ham, chopped
85g/3oz mature cheddar cheese
85g/3oz dolcelatte or other
blue cheese
85g/3oz garlic and herb soft cheese
85g/3oz mixed nuts, such as
cashews, blanched almonds
and hazelnuts, roughly chopped
handful of parsley,
roughly chopped

Takes about 1 hour • Serves 4

1 Cook the pasta in a large pan of salted boiling water for 8–10 minutes, or according to the packet instructions, until just tender. Preheat the oven to 190°C/Gas 5/fan oven 170°C.
2 Pour the milk into a pan and add the butter, flour and seasoning. Grate in the ½ nutmeg (or sprinkle in the ground). Bring to the boil over a medium heat, whisking until it makes a smooth, creamy sauce.
3 Drain the pasta and tip it into the sauce. Stir in the ham and grate in the cheddar, then taste for seasoning and tip into a shallow ovenproof dish. Dice the remaining cheeses and swirl into the pasta to make cheesy pockets. Scatter the nuts and parsley over the top, then bake for 30 minutes.

• Per serving 840 kcalories, protein 55g, carbohydrate 26g, fat 44g, saturated fat 21g, fibre 6g, added sugar none, salt 2.61g

Don't be put off by the time it takes to roast the tomatoes and aubergines – it's well worth it for the extra flavour.

Pasta Parmigiana

1.25kg/2lb 12oz small vine or plum tomatoes, halved crossways
sprinkling of golden caster sugar
4 tbsp extra virgin olive oil, plus extra for drizzling and brushing
1 large aubergine (about 450g/1lb)
500g/1lb 2oz rigatoni or penne
2 garlic cloves, crushed
2 good handfuls of basil leaves, plus extra for serving
450g/1lb buffalo mozzarella cheese (3 balls), drained and very thinly sliced
50g/2oz parmesan cheese, freshly grated

Takes 2½ hours • Serves 6

1 Preheat the oven to 160°C/Gas 3/fan oven 140°C. Stand the tomatoes cut-side up on a large baking tray and sprinkle with the sugar and seasoning. Drizzle with oil and roast for 45 minutes. Meanwhile, slice the aubergine into rounds, brush both sides with oil and spread out on another tray. When the tomatoes have been roasting for 45 minutes, put the aubergine in the oven and roast for another 45 minutes.
2 Cook the pasta, drain well and mix in a bowl with 4 tablespoons oil and the garlic. Remove the vegetables from the oven and turn it up to 200°C/Gas 6/fan oven 180°C. Layer the pasta and vegetables with the basil and mozzarella in a 2.5-litre/3½–4-pint oven-proof dish, finishing with a layer of tomatoes and mozzarella and then the parmesan. Bake for 25 minutes and serve sprinkled with basil.

• Per serving 722 kcalories, protein 29g, carbohydrate 73g, fat 37g, saturated fat 16g, fibre 7g, added sugar 2g, salt 2.07g

Quark, a low-fat soft cheese, and skimmed milk replace the conventional calorific béchamel sauce in this lean, yet tasty lasagne.

Pork and Rosemary Lasagne

1 tsp olive oil, plus extra for greasing
400g/14oz lean minced pork
1 onion, finely chopped
2 celery sticks, finely chopped
1 tsp dried rosemary
150ml/¼ pint white wine
425ml/¾ pint chicken stock
2 tbsp tomato purée
400g can chopped tomatoes
1 tsp cornflour, mixed to a paste
with a little cold water
2 × 250g cartons quark
250ml/9fl oz skimmed milk
freshly grated nutmeg
10 dried lasagne sheets
(no pre-cooking required type)
15g/½oz freshly grated parmesan
cheese (about 5 tbsp)

Takes about 1½ hours • Serves 4

1 Heat the oil in a non-stick pan and fry the pork until brown and crumbly. Add the onion, celery, rosemary and wine, simmer for 10 minutes, then stir in the stock, purée and tomatoes. Season, cover and simmer for 30 minutes. Stir in the cornflour paste until slightly thickened, then remove from the heat.
2 Preheat the oven to 190°C/Gas 5/fan oven 170°C. Mix the quark with the milk, nutmeg and seasoning. Spoon a third of the meat over the base of a 1.4-litre/2½-pint oblong baking dish. Cover with 2 lasagne sheets, avoiding overlapping. Top with a third of the sauce and a little parmesan, then 2 more lasagne sheets. Repeat the layers twice more, omitting the last layer of lasagne and finishing with sauce. Sprinkle with the remaining parmesan and bake for 30–35 minutes.

• Per serving 425 kcalories, protein 41g, carbohydrate 45g, fat 7g, saturated fat 2g, fibre 3g, added sugar none, salt 1.03g

The perfect dish for a spoil-yourself Saturday night supper – it's easy to cook, tastes really special and only needs a simple salad to go with it.

Salmon and Broccoli Pasta Bake

250g/9oz penne
300g/10oz broccoli florets
25g/1oz butter
25g/1oz plain flour
600ml/1 pint milk
100g/4oz mascarpone cheese
8 sun-dried tomatoes (preserved in oil), drained and thickly sliced
10 large fresh basil leaves, roughly torn
4 fresh skinless salmon fillets, halved widthways
50g/2oz mature cheddar cheese, finely grated

Takes about 1 hour • Serves 4

1 Preheat the oven to 190°C/Gas 5/fan oven 170°C. Cook the pasta in salted boiling water for 6 minutes, add the broccoli and boil for another 4 minutes.
2 Meanwhile, put the butter, flour and milk in a pan and simmer, whisking, to make a thick, smooth sauce. Remove from the heat and stir in the mascarpone, tomatoes and basil.
3 Drain the pasta and broccoli, mix with the sauce and season well. Put the salmon in a single layer in an ovenproof dish (30 × 20 × 6cm/12 × 8 × 2½in), spoon the pasta mixture on top and scatter with the cheese. Bake for 30 minutes until golden.

• Per serving 817 kcalories, protein 49g, carbohydrate 64g, fat 42g, saturated fat 18g, fibre 5g, added sugar none, salt 1.3g

You can serve this vegetarian pasta bake
hot or cold.

Easy Oven Pasta Frittata

½ tsp olive oil
85g/3oz fusilli or macaroni
1 leek or 1 bunch of spring onions,
chopped
85g/3oz frozen or canned sweetcorn
85g/3oz frozen peas
1 red pepper, seeded and chopped
2 large eggs
150ml/¼ pint semi-skimmed milk
1 tbsp fresh thyme leaves
50g/2oz extra mature cheddar
cheese, grated
2 tbsp freshly grated parmesan
cheese

Takes about 1 hour • Serves 4

1 Preheat the oven to 190°C/Gas 5/fan oven 170°C. Grease a 1.2-litre/2-pint ovenproof dish with the oil.
2 Cook the pasta in a large pan of salted boiling water for 8 minutes. Add the vegetables and cook for another 2–3 minutes until the pasta is tender and the vegetables slightly softened. Drain, then tip into the prepared dish and stir together.
3 Beat the eggs, milk and thyme in a jug. Mix in the cheddar and seasoning to taste. Pour into the dish, stir gently, then scatter the parmesan on top. Bake for 35–40 minutes until set and golden.

• Per serving 277 kcalories, protein 16g, carbohydrate 29g, fat 12g, saturated fat 6g, fibre 3g, added sugar 2g, salt 0.7g

A great idea for a special veggie treat –
perfect for family get-togethers.

Roasted Vegetable Lasagne

2 red peppers, seeded and
roughly chopped
2 courgettes, roughly chopped
2 red onions, roughly chopped
1 aubergine, roughly chopped
6 garlic cloves, peeled
3 tbsp olive oil
280g jar roasted artichoke hearts
in oil, drained
2 × 300g cartons fresh arrabbiata
sauce
2 × 250g cartons ricotta cheese
2 eggs, beaten
6 tbsp milk
140g/5oz parmesan cheese,
freshly grated
8 sheets fresh lasagne, or dried
(no pre-cooking required type)
25g/1oz cheddar cheese, grated

Takes about 1½ hours • Serves 6

1 Preheat the oven to 200°C/Gas 6/fan oven 180°C. Put the peppers, courgettes, onions, aubergine and garlic in a large shallow roasting tin. Drizzle with the oil and season well. Roast, stirring occasionally, for 30–40 minutes. Transfer to a bowl (leaving the oven on) and stir in the artichokes and arrabbiata sauce. Season to taste.
2 In a bowl, beat together the ricotta, eggs, milk, parmesan and seasoning. Set aside.
3 Spoon a third of the vegetables over the base of a lightly greased shallow ovenproof dish (33 × 19 × 9cm/13 × 7½ × 3½in). Cover with one third of the lasagne. Repeat these layers twice more, then spread with the ricotta mixture and sprinkle with the cheddar. Bake for 30–40 minutes or until golden brown and bubbling.

• Per serving 503 kcalories, protein 28g, carbohydrate 29g, fat 31g, saturated fat 14g, fibre 5g, added sugar 3g, salt 3.19g

This robust family favourite is great for serving up after a long country walk in winter.

Golden Macaroni Cheese

200g/8oz macaroni
85g/3oz butter
50g/2oz plain flour
350ml/12fl oz hot milk
142ml carton whipping cream
175g/6oz extra mature cheddar
cheese, grated
1 tsp Dijon mustard
50g/2oz parmesan cheese, grated
1 large onion, thinly sliced
1 tbsp olive oil

Takes 40 minutes • Serves 4

1 Preheat the oven to 180°C/Gas 4/fan oven 160°C. Cook the macaroni according to the packet instructions, until tender. Meanwhile, melt two thirds of the butter in a medium pan, sprinkle in the flour and cook, stirring, for 1 minute. Remove from the heat and gradually whisk in the milk and cream, then return to the heat and bring to the boil, stirring. Simmer and stir for 5 minutes, until thickened and smooth, then remove from the heat and stir in the cheddar, mustard and half the parmesan.
2 Drain the pasta and mix with the sauce and seasoning. Turn into a 1.2-litre/2-pint ovenproof dish, sprinkle over the remaining parmesan and bake for 20 minutes. Meanwhile, cook the onion in the oil and the remaining butter until golden brown. Sprinkle over the macaroni before serving.

• Per serving 829 kcalories, protein 27g, carbohydrate 57g, fat 56g, saturated fat 33.1g, fibre 2.6g, added sugar none, salt 1.6g

This surprisingly light pasta bake is quick and straightforward, and makes an impressive veggie supper.

Ricotta Pasta Pockets

250g pack fresh lasagne sheets
1 tbsp olive oil
250g carton ricotta cheese
50g bag rocket
2 × 350g jars tomato and chargrilled vegetable sauce, or your favourite tomato sauce
50g/2oz mature vegetarian cheddar cheese, grated

Takes 30 minutes • Serves 4

1 Put the lasagne sheets in a large bowl and pour over boiling water to cover. Leave to soak for 5 minutes. Meanwhile, preheat the oven to 200°C/Gas 6/fan oven 180°C and lightly oil a shallow baking tray.

2 Drain the lasagne in a colander. Take one sheet and put a large spoonful of ricotta in the centre. Scatter over a few rocket leaves and season well, then fold the sheet in half and press the edges together to form a pocket. Continue to fill all the pasta sheets, then lay them on the baking tray so they overlap slightly.

3 Cover the pasta pockets with the sauce, sprinkle over the cheese and bake for 10–12 minutes until hot and bubbly.

• Per serving 440 kcalories, protein 19g, carbohydrate 57g, fat 17g, saturated fat 8g, fibre 4g, added sugar 5g, salt 3.5g

As with all soufflé-type mixtures, make sure this family supper dish is eaten as soon as it's ready as it will sink within minutes.

Cheddar and Spaghetti Puff

50g/2oz spaghetti, broken into finger lengths
50g/2oz butter
3 tbsp dried breadcrumbs
25g/1oz plain flour
½ tsp mustard powder
250ml/9fl oz hot milk
1 large spring onion, trimmed and finely chopped
25g/1oz baby spinach or rocket leaves, shredded
3 medium eggs, separated, plus 1 extra white
140g/5oz mature cheddar cheese, coarsely grated

Takes 1–1¼ hours • Serves 3–4

1 Preheat the oven to 190°C/Gas 5/fan oven 170°C with a baking sheet on the centre shelf. Cook the spaghetti according to the packet instructions until tender, then drain.
2 Melt the butter in a pan. Brush a little inside a 1.2-litre/2-pint soufflé dish, then coat with the breadcrumbs. Stir the flour and mustard into the butter and cook for 1 minute. Gradually whisk in the milk. Simmer until you have a smooth sauce. Remove from the heat and stir in the onion, leaves, spaghetti, egg yolks and cheese, keeping 2 tablespoons to one side.
3 Whisk the egg whites to the floppy peak stage, beat a quarter into the soufflé mix; fold in the rest. Spoon into the dish, make a gully all around the edge with your thumb and sprinkle over the reserved cheese. Bake on the hot tray for 30–35 minutes until risen and golden.

• Per serving for four 436 kcalories, protein 20g, carbohydrate 26g, fat 29g, saturated fat 16g, fibre 0.7g, added sugar none, salt 1.21g

This fragrant Thai soup, known as *tom yum*, can be made with pieces of shredded chicken instead of prawns, if you prefer.

Spicy Prawn Noodle Soup

900ml/1½ pints chicken stock
2 lemon grass stalks, bruised with a rolling pin
2.5cm/1in piece of fresh ginger, peeled and finely chopped
1 fresh green chilli, seeded and finely chopped
2 garlic cloves, finely chopped
100g/4oz medium egg noodles
2 tbsp Thai fish sauce, plus more to taste
juice of ½ lime
pinch of sugar
12 peeled raw tiger prawns, with tail shells left on
1 small bunch of fresh coriander, roughly chopped, with 4 whole sprigs reserved
lime wedges, to serve

Takes 25 minutes • Serves 4

1 Bring the stock to the boil in a large saucepan with the lemon grass, ginger, chilli and garlic, then add the noodles and simmer for 4 minutes.

2 Now stir in 2 tablespoons fish sauce, the lime juice and sugar followed by the prawns. Simmer for 3–4 minutes until the prawns turn pink.

3 Remove the pan from the heat and throw in the chopped coriander. Stir and taste for seasoning, adding more fish sauce if you like. Serve straight away, with the reserved coriander sprigs as a garnish and lime wedges for squeezing.

• Per serving 145 kcalories, protein 12g, carbohydrate 20g, fat 2g, saturated fat 0.1g, fibre 0.1g, added sugar 0.7g, salt 2.51g

Just throw everything into a pan, leave it to simmer briefly and – hey presto – your supper for one is ready.

Aromatic Soy Pork

150ml/¼ pint chicken stock
2 tbsp soy sauce
1 tbsp dry sherry
1 tsp Chinese five-spice powder or 2 tsp five-spice paste
2.5cm/1in piece fresh ginger, peeled and finely sliced
1 garlic clove, finely sliced
½ bunch (about 4) spring onions, trimmed and left whole
140–175g/5–6oz pork tenderloin, sliced into long thin strips
about 50g/2oz flat rice noodles
drizzle of sesame or vegetable oil
1 tsp sesame seeds, toasted
1 small bok choi or a few Chinese cabbage leaves, cut widthways into 2.5cm/1in slices
handful of coriander leaves

Takes 35–45 minutes • Serves 1

1 Put the stock, soy sauce, sherry, five-spice powder (or paste), ginger, garlic and spring onions into a small saucepan with a lid and bring to a gentle simmer. After about 2 minutes, stir in the pork, cover and let it simmer away, but not boil, for about 5 minutes.
2 Put the noodles in a bowl with boiling water and soak for 4 minutes. Drain the noodles and toss with the oil and sesame seeds.
3 When the pork is ready, stir in the bok choi or Chinese cabbage and simmer for 1 minute. To serve, pile the noodles into a bowl, spoon the pork and other bits on the top, pour the broth around and scatter the coriander leaves over. And don't forget to keep paper napkins handy for those noodle slurps.

• Per serving 622 kcalories, protein 37g, carbohydrate 48g, fat 31g, saturated fat 10g, fibre 2g, added sugar 1g, salt 6.18g

A wonderful, authentic Thai classic. If there are two thicknesses of
noodle on offer, go for the thicker ones for this recipe.

Pad Thai

125g (½ × 250g pack) rice noodles
3 tbsp lime juice (about 2 limes)
½ tsp cayenne pepper
2 tsp light muscovado sugar
2 tbsp Thai fish sauce
2 tbsp vegetable oil
200g/8oz cooked peeled tiger
prawns, tail shells left on
4 spring onions, sliced
140g/5oz beansprouts
25g/1oz salted peanuts,
finely chopped
small handful of coriander leaves

TO SERVE
1–2 limes, cut into wedges
sweet chilli sauce

Takes 25–30 minutes • Serves 2–3

1 Put the noodles in a large heatproof bowl,
pour boiling water over them and leave
for 4 minutes, then drain and refresh under
cold running water.
2 Put the lime juice, cayenne, sugar and
fish sauce in a bowl and mix well. Have all
the other ingredients ready by the cooker.
3 Heat the oil and fry the prawns until
warmed through. Add the spring onions and
noodles and toss to mix. Tip in the lime juice
mixture, then stir in the beansprouts and half
the peanuts and coriander. Cook for 1 minute
until everything is heated through.
4 Pile into a large dish, scatter with the rest
of the peanuts and coriander, and serve with
lime wedges and chilli sauce.

• Per serving for two 531 kcalories, protein 27g,
carbohydrate 62g, fat 20g, saturated fat 3g, fibre 2g,
added sugar 5g, salt 3g

Dried mushrooms give the same deep taste as soy sauce but,
as they are virtually salt-free, they are much healthier.

Oriental Beef and Mushroom Soup

25g/1oz dried ceps or
porcini mushrooms
½ beef stock cube
1 tbsp sunflower oil
1 extra-lean sirloin steak,
about 140g/5oz
1 fresh red chilli, seeded and
finely chopped
2 garlic cloves, crushed
1 tsp finely grated fresh ginger
100g/4oz small broccoli florets,
halved
2 tbsp dry sherry
100g/4oz fine egg noodles
100g/4oz fresh beansprouts
25g/1oz watercress,
roughly chopped

Takes 20–30 minutes • Serves 2

1 Snip the mushrooms into a large measuring jug, pour over 1 litre/1¾ pints boiling water and crumble in the stock cube. Set aside.
2 Heat the oil in a large non-stick pan. Add the steak and cook over a high heat for 2 minutes on each side. Lift on to a plate.
3 Add the chilli, garlic and ginger to the pan with the broccoli and stir fry for about a minute. Spoon in the sherry and stir to remove any sediment from the pan. Pour in the stock and mushrooms and simmer for 4 minutes.
4 Pour a kettleful of boiling water over the noodles in a large bowl and leave to soften. Add the beansprouts and watercress to the soup and cook for 2 minutes. Drain the noodles, divide between two soup bowls, then ladle over the soup. Thinly slice the beef and pile on top.

• Per serving 488 kcalories, protein 30g, carbohydrate 48g, fat 15g, saturated fat 2g, fibre 2g, added sugar none, salt 2.26g

Try to buy rice paper wrappers from oriental stores – supermaket wrappers tend to be smaller, so you'll need twice as many.

Tiger Prawn Spring Rolls

4 large iceberg lettuce leaves, halved lengthways, with crunchy cores cut out
8 round sheets of rice paper, 23cm/9in in diameter
8 each fresh mint and coriander leaves
soy sauce, for dipping

FOR THE FILLING
25g/1oz rice vermicelli noodles
175g/6oz peeled raw tiger prawns
2.5cm/1in piece of fresh ginger, peeled and finely chopped
1 garlic clove, finely chopped
1 tbsp vegetable oil
1 medium carrot, grated
50g/2oz beansprouts
handful each of fresh mint and coriander leaves, chopped

Takes about 1 hour • Serves 6

1 First make the filling. Soak the noodles until soft, then drain. Chop the prawns, then stir fry them with the ginger and garlic in hot oil for 2–3 minutes until the prawns turn pink. Tip into a bowl and stir in the remaining filling ingredients, then pile into the lettuce halves and roll them up.
2 One at a time, dip the rice paper sheets in hot water for 30–40 seconds until soft. Lay them on damp tea towels and put a mint and coriander leaf on each one. Now put a lettuce roll just off centre on each rice paper sheet and roll it up, tucking in the sides halfway.
3 Keep the rolls wrapped, seam-side down, in the damp tea towels. Just before serving, unwrap and cut each roll at an angle. Serve with soy sauce for dipping.

• Per serving 75 kcalories, protein 7g, carbohydrate 8g, fat 2g, saturated fat 0.2g, fibre 0.7g, added sugar 0.1g, salt 1.55g

This complete meal in a wok is great for a weekday supper.
Straight-to-wok noodles will save you time as well.

Spring Vegetable Noodles

2 tbsp olive oil
3 smoked back bacon rashers
250g/9oz green vegetables, such as
fine asparagus and broccoli,
cut into bite-sized pieces,
and frozen petits pois
2 garlic cloves, finely sliced
6 spring onions, trimmed, halved
lengthways and quartered
150g pack straight-to-wok noodles
soy sauce, to serve

Takes 20–25 minutes • Serves 2

1 Heat the oil in a wok. Using scissors, snip the bacon into the hot oil and fry, stirring occasionally, for 2 minutes.
2 Tip in the asparagus and broccoli with the garlic and spring onions. Stir fry for about a minute, then top with the noodles and peas and drizzle over 1 tablespoon water. Cover the pan and let everything steam for 4 minutes until the broccoli is just tender.
3 Mix everything together and serve straight away, with soy sauce for sprinkling.

• Per serving 339 kcalories, protein 15g, carbohydrate 27g, fat 20g, saturated fat 4g, fibre 5g, added sugar none, salt 2.21g

This Chinese dish, using mainly storecupboard ingredients, is easy to whip up for an impromptu supper with friends.

Pork and Noodle Stir Fry

2 tbsp sunflower oil
250g/9oz pork fillet, trimmed and cut into strips
½ bunch of spring onions, trimmed and sliced on the diagonal
100g/4oz mangetout, cut lengthways into strips
150g pack straight-to-wok noodles

FOR THE SAUCE
2 tsp cornflour
juice of 1 large orange
3 tbsp soy sauce
2 tbsp rice wine or sherry
1 tbsp clear honey

Takes 30 minutes • Serves 2

1 First get the sauce ready. Mix the cornflour with 6 tablespoons water in a jug and stir in the remaining ingredients. Set aside.
2 Heat the oil in a wok and stir fry the pork over a high heat until coloured on all sides, about 5 minutes. Lower the heat, toss in the onions and mangetout and stir fry for about 5 minutes to soften.
3 Stir the sauce in the jug, pour into the pan and stir briskly to mix. Bubble for a few minutes, toss in the noodles and heat through. Serve straight away.

• Per serving 490 kcalories, protein 34g, carbohydrate 40g, fat 21g, saturated fat 4.4g, fibre 2.5g, added sugar 6.2g, salt 4.98g

A salad mix that includes carrot, pepper and cabbage
will add crunch to this tasty and healthy soup.

Oriental Leaf and Noodle Broth

2 litres/3½ pints vegetable stock
1 tsp grated fresh ginger
100g/4oz button mushrooms,
thinly sliced
100g/4oz rice noodles
4 spring onions, trimmed and sliced
250g bag sweet and crunchy salad
(white cabbage, carrots, lettuce,
red and green peppers)
juice of 1 lime

Takes 10 minutes • Serves 4

1 Bring the stock and ginger to the boil in
a large saucepan. Stir in the mushrooms and
noodles and simmer gently for 2 minutes
until the noodles are almost tender.
2 Tip in the spring onions and salad and
simmer for 30 seconds, then stir in the lime
juice and seasoning to taste. Serve straight
away.

• Per serving 117 kcalories, protein 6g, carbohydrate
23g, fat 1g, saturated fat 0.1g, fibre 1.4g, added
sugar none, salt 1.66g

Don't worry if your prawn cakes aren't piping hot – most Thai food is served warm and it means you can savour the flavours better.

Prawn Cakes with Spicy Noodles

3 tbsp sunflower oil
140g/5oz medium egg noodles
1 garlic clove, crushed
1 rounded tsp grated fresh ginger
1 small fresh red chilli, seeded and finely chopped
50g/2oz mangetout, trimmed and thinly sliced lengthways
2 spring onions, trimmed and sliced on the diagonal
2 tbsp soy sauce
1 tbsp sesame seeds, toasted
1 tbsp chopped fresh coriander

FOR THE PRAWN CAKES
1 spring onion
1 small fresh red chilli
2 tbsp chopped fresh coriander
200g/8oz peeled raw tiger prawns
1–2 tbsp plain flour, for coating

Takes 50 minutes • Serves 2

1 First make the prawn cakes. Trim and roughly chop the spring onion and seed and half the chilli lengthways. Chop them to a coarse paste in a food processor with the coriander and some salt. Add the prawns and chop again, leaving some texture. Shape into four 1cm/½in thick rounds and coat with flour. Heat 2 tablespoons of the oil in a frying pan. Fry the cakes over a medium heat for 3–4 minutes on each side, until golden.
2 Meanwhile, cook the noodles according to the packet instructions. Heat the remaining oil in a wok and stir fry the garlic, ginger and chilli for 1 minute. Tip in the mangetout and onions, stir fry for 2 minutes, then remove from the heat. Drain the noodles and toss into the stir fry with the soy sauce. Serve topped with the prawn cakes, sesame seeds and coriander.

• Per serving 621 kcalories, protein 33g, carbohydrate 61g, fat 29g, saturated fat 4g, fibre 2g, added sugar 1g, salt 3.59g

Add this simple but tasty dish to your repertoire and you'll never have to rely on takeaways again.

Noodles with Black Bean Pork

2 tbsp vegetable oil
2 garlic cloves, crushed
2cm/¾in piece of fresh ginger,
peeled and grated
1 large fresh red chilli, seeded and
finely chopped
450g/1lb minced pork
350g jar black bean sauce
100g/4oz rice noodles
6 spring onions, trimmed
and shredded

Takes 35 minutes • Serves 4

1 Heat the oil in a large pan and cook the garlic, ginger and chilli gently for 1–2 minutes until softened. Add the pork and cook for 4–5 minutes until browned, pressing with a spoon to remove any lumps. Pour in the black bean sauce and stir well, then cook for another 4–5 minutes, stirring occasionally.
2 Meanwhile, cook or soak the rice noodles according to the packet instructions. Drain and toss into the pork with the spring onions. Serve straight away.

• Per serving 405 kcalories, protein 31g, carbohydrate 31g, fat 18g, saturated fat 5.3g, fibre 2g, added sugar 3.9g, salt 5.78g

Rice vermicelli are very fine noodles that are low in fat
and also wheat- and gluten-free.

Stir-fried Greens and Vermicelli

100g/4oz rice vermicelli
1 tbsp soy sauce
1 tbsp Thai fish sauce
3 tbsp oyster sauce
2 tbsp sunflower oil
4 spring onions, trimmed
and chopped
3 garlic cloves, chopped
1 fresh red chilli, seeded
and chopped
100g/4oz shiitake or chestnut
mushrooms, sliced
200g/8oz broccoli florets
2 heads pak choi, roughly chopped

Takes 20 minutes • Serves 3

1 Soak the vermicelli in boiling water for
4 minutes. Drain, refresh under cold running
water, drain again and set aside.
2 Mix the sauces together in a bowl. Heat
the oil in a large wok and stir fry the spring
onions, garlic and chilli for 20 seconds.
3 Add the mushrooms and broccoli to the
wok. Stir fry for 1 minute, then add the pak
choi and the sauce mixture. Stir fry for about
2 minutes, adding a splash of water if the
sauce becomes too thick. Toss in the noodles
and heat through before serving.

• Per serving 241 kcalories, protein 10g, carbohydrate
34g, fat 8g, saturated fat 1g, fibre 2.5g, added sugar
1.1g, salt 3.85g

Stir fry rice noodles are soft, silky and
delicate once cooked.

Chinese Noodle Soup

100g/4oz (2 bundles) stir fry noodles
1.2 litres/2 pints good-quality
chicken stock
2 kaffir lime leaves, finely shredded
1 tsp grated fresh ginger
2 tbsp finely chopped fresh
coriander
418g can creamed-style corn
2 cooked chicken breasts, skinned,
boned and shredded

Takes 20 minutes • Serves 4

1 Soak the noodles in boiling water for
4 minutes. Drain, rinse and drain again,
then divide between four soup bowls.
2 Heat the stock to boiling in a saucepan
with the lime leaves, ginger and coriander.
3 Add the sweetcorn and chicken to the
pan, stir and heat through for 2 minutes,
then ladle over the noodles.

• Per serving 350 kcalories, protein 24g, carbohydrate
59g, fat 3g, saturated fat 0.9g, fibre 1.7g, added
sugar 7.7g, salt 2.68g

Treat yourself to this exciting East-meets-West stir fry. It's ideal for one person as you only use one pan and it's so quick and easy.

Chicken Noodle Stir Fry

finely grated zest and juice of
1 orange
1 tbsp clear honey
1 tsp soy sauce, plus extra to serve
2.5cm/1in piece of fresh ginger,
peeled and chopped
to a pulp or grated
1 garlic clove, finely chopped
or grated
¼ packet stir fry rice noodles
2 handfuls of spinach leaves,
roughly chopped
1 tbsp sesame oil
1 tbsp vegetable oil
1 large boneless skinless chicken
breast, sliced into strips
sprinkling of chilli flakes

Takes 25 minutes • Serves 1

1 Whisk the orange zest and juice in a bowl with the honey, soy sauce, ginger and garlic.
2 Soak the noodles in boiling water for 4 minutes. Put the spinach in a colander in the sink. Slowly pour the noodles and water over the spinach, then toss until the spinach wilts. Drizzle over the sesame oil and mix gently.
3 Heat the vegetable oil in a wok until very hot and fry the chicken over a high heat for 5 minutes until golden brown. Pour in the orange mixture, then bubble and stir for 2 minutes until a shiny glaze forms over the chicken.
4 Tip the noodles, spinach and chilli flakes into the wok and toss gently together until hot. Season and serve straight away, with soy sauce at the table.

• Per serving 721 kcalories, protein 44g, carbohydrate 85g, fat 25g, saturated fat 4g, fibre 3g, added sugar 12g, salt 1.4g

Take advantage of fresh asparagus when it's in season with this flavour-packed stir fry.

Asparagus and Pepper Noodles

1 tbsp sesame seeds
2 portions dried egg noodles
(about 175g/6oz in total)
2 tsp toasted sesame oil
1 tbsp sunflower oil
1 small fresh red chilli, seeded and
finely chopped
1 tbsp finely chopped fresh ginger
1 red pepper, seeded and
cut into chunks
100g pack asparagus tips
2 garlic cloves, thinly sliced
½ bunch of spring onions, trimmed
and chopped
½ tsp five-spice powder
½ tsp light muscovado sugar
2 tsp soy sauce

Takes 35–45 minutes • Serves 2

1 Heat a wok over a medium to high heat and dry fry the sesame seeds, swirling them constantly until toasty. Tip them out and set aside.

2 Cook the noodles according to the packet instructions. Drain well and toss with the sesame oil.

3 Heat the sunflower oil in the wok and stir fry the chilli and ginger for 30 seconds. Add the red pepper and fry for a few minutes, then tip in the asparagus and garlic and fry for 2 minutes. Add the onions, five-spice, sugar and soy with 4 tablespoons water and stir vigorously, then toss in the noodles and sesame seeds and mix thoroughly until hot. Serve immediately.

• Per serving 523 kcalories, protein 15g, carbohydrate 73g, fat 21g, saturated fat 2.2g, fibre 3.2g, added sugar 1.4g, salt 1.33g

Alternatively you can use peeled raw tiger prawns, but only sauté for 30 seconds–1 minute until they turn pink.

Tofu and Vegetable Stir Fry

350g/12oz firm tofu,
cut into 2cm/¾in cubes
1 tbsp light soy sauce
1 tbsp chilli sauce
1 tsp sesame oil
50g/2oz egg noodles
1 tbsp vegetable oil
200g/8oz pak choi or spinach
1 red pepper, seeded and cubed
6 spring onions, trimmed and cut
into 5cm/2in lengths
85g/3oz mangetout
1 tbsp cashew nuts,
roughly chopped

Takes 30 minutes • Serves 2

1 Marinate the tofu with the soy, chilli sauce and sesame oil. Cook the noodles in a large pan of salted boiling water for 4 minutes or until tender, drain then return to the pan.
2 Heat the vegetable oil in a wok or large frying pan until really hot, then stir fry the tofu for 2–3 minutes until golden. Tip into the noodles.
3 Cut off the pak choi leaves and chop the stems on a slant. Add the stems to the wok with the pepper, spring onions, mangetout and cashew nuts and stir fry for 3–4 minutes until softened.
4 Return the noodles and tofu to the wok. Throw in the pak choi leaves or spinach, toss thoroughly and serve.

• Per serving 403 kcalories, protein 23g, carbohydrate 33g, fat 21g, saturated fat 2g, fibre 3g, added sugar 1g, salt 3.89g

Make the most of quick-cooking ingredients to create an appetizing stir fry. For vegetarians, replace the pork with mushrooms.

Pork and Ginger Noodles

2 tbsp sunflower oil
450g/1lb pork fillet, cut into thin strips about 1cm/½in wide
2.5cm/1in piece of fresh ginger, grated
2 garlic cloves, finely chopped
½ Savoy cabbage, about 250g/9oz, shredded
300ml/½ pint vegetable or chicken stock
1 tbsp soy sauce
100g/4oz frozen peas
2 × 150g packs straight-to-wok noodles
2 tbsp chopped fresh coriander, to serve

Takes 25 minutes • Serves 4

1 Heat the oil in a wok over a high heat, add the pork and stir fry for 3–4 minutes until just cooked. Stir in the ginger and garlic and continue to fry for 1–2 minutes.
2 Add the cabbage and stir fry with the pork until well combined. Pour over the stock and soy sauce.
3 Add the peas and noodles, stir well, then simmer for 5 minutes, until the cabbage is cooked but still crunchy. Scatter with coriander and serve.

• Per serving 337 kcalories, protein 31g, carbohydrate 28g, fat 12g, saturated fat 2g, fibre 4g, added sugar none, salt 1.84g

This hearty winter soup, packed with fibre, is a deliciously simple way of ensuring you and your family get your daily quota of vegetables.

Winter Minestrone

2 tbsp olive oil
1 leek, cut into bite-sized chunks
175g/6oz carrots, cut into
bite-sized chunks
3–4 celery sticks, cut into
bite-sized chunks
1 garlic clove, chopped
1.5 litres/2¾ pints vegetable stock or
boiling water
1 bay leaf
175g/6oz potatoes, cut into chunks
2 × 400g cans chopped tomatoes
50g/2oz soup pasta,
such as vermicelli
3 tbsp chopped fresh parsley
400g can cannellini beans, drained
and rinsed
85g/3oz frozen peas
freshly grated parmesan cheese,
to serve

Takes 50 minutes • Serves 6

1 Heat the oil in a large heavy-based pan. Add the leek, carrots and celery. Cook for 2–3 minutes, stir in the garlic and cook for 1 minute more.
2 Add the stock or water, bay leaf, potatoes and tomatoes. Bring to the boil, then cover and simmer gently for 10 minutes.
3 Season to taste, stir in the pasta and parsley and cook for a further 10–15 minutes, or until the pasta and vegetables are almost tender. Add the beans and peas and cook for 3–4 minutes. Serve with freshly grated parmesan.

• Per serving 279 kcalories, protein 16g, carbohydrate 44g, fat 6g, saturated fat 1g, fibre 12g, added sugar none, salt 1.07g

Chinese five-spice powder is an aromatic mix of salt, pepper, star anise, cinnamon, cloves, ginger and garlic.

One-pot Chicken Noodles

4 skinless boneless chicken breasts
2 large carrots, peeled
2 tbsp vegetable oil
½ tsp five-spice powder
1 litre/1¾ pints hot chicken stock, made with 2 cubes
198g can sweetcorn niblets, drained, or 175g/6oz frozen sweetcorn kernels
175g/6oz frozen peas or petits pois
2 good splashes of soy sauce, plus extra for serving, to taste
½ × 250g pack rice noodles, broken in half
1 bunch of salad or spring onions

Takes 30–40 minutes • Serves 4

1 Cut the chicken into short strips. Cut the carrots into the same size sticks. Heat the oil in a large pan and tip in the carrots, chicken, five-spice and seasoning. Sizzle for 5 minutes until the chicken is opaque.
2 Pour in the stock and bring to the boil. Stir well, cover and simmer for 10 minutes. Stir in the sweetcorn, peas and soy sauce, and heat through for a few minutes.
3 Meanwhile, soak the noodles in boiling water for 4 minutes. Slice the salad or spring onions on the diagonal.
4 Drain the noodles and tip into the pan of chicken and vegetables, along with the salad or spring onions. Stir gently and taste for seasoning, adding more soy sauce if you like.

• Per serving 411 kcalories, protein 41g, carbohydrate 44g, fat 9g, saturated fat 1g, fibre 5g, added sugar none, salt 2.05g

Sweet cherry peppers are available in some larger supermarkets – if you can't find them, use sliced peppers from a jar.

Sweet Pepper Pasta

350g/12oz trompetti or fusilli
2 tsp olive oil
1 large onion, roughly chopped
2 plump garlic cloves, crushed
375g jar mild Peppadew sweet cherry peppers
85g bag rocket or watercress, roughly torn

Takes 20 minutes • Serves 4

1 Cook the pasta in a large pan of salted boiling water for 8–10 minutes, or according to the packet instructions, until tender.
2 Meanwhile, heat the oil in a large pan and fry the onion over a medium-high heat for 5–6 minutes, until golden and softened. Stir in the garlic and cook for a further 2–3 minutes. Drain the peppers, reserving their juice, and stir them into the onion. Cook for 2–3 minutes. Blitz the mixture in a food processor with 5 tablespoons each reserved pepper juice and pasta cooking water.
3 Drain the pasta and return it to the pan with the pepper mixture and seasoning to taste. Toss in the rocket or watercress and heat through briefly until it just begins to wilt. Serve straight away.

• Per serving 375 kcalories, protein 13g, carbohydrate 77g, fat 4g, saturated fat 1g, fibre 6g, added sugar none, salt trace

To vary the flavour, stir in a handful of small spinach leaves
or beansprouts right at the end.

Chicken Noodle Soup

3 tbsp soy sauce
1 garlic clove, thinly sliced
2.5cm/1in piece of fresh ginger,
peeled and grated
2 carrots, peeled and cut into sticks
2 skinless boneless chicken breasts,
cut into thin strips
2 leeks, cut into strips
175g/6oz chestnut mushrooms,
sliced
85g/3oz egg noodles

Takes 20 minutes • Serves 4

1 Pour the soy sauce and 1.3 litres/2¼ pints hot water into a pan. Add the garlic, ginger, carrots and chicken strips. Bring to the boil, then simmer for 5 minutes.
2 Throw in the leeks, mushrooms and noodles and simmer for 4 minutes or until the noodles are tender. Season and serve in bowls.

• Per serving 203 kcalories, protein 22g, carbohydrate 23g, fat 3g, saturated fat none, fibre 3g, added sugar none, salt 2.53g

A great vegetarian family recipe that you can
whip up in no time at all.

Pasta with Cherry Tomato Sauce

450g/1lb cherry tomatoes
pinch of golden caster sugar
1 onion, chopped
2 garlic cloves, crushed
1 tsp dried or 1 tbsp chopped fresh
oregano, plus extra to garnish
5 tbsp vegetable stock
350g/12oz short pasta shapes,
such as penne or penne rigate

Takes 20 minutes • Serves 4

1 Put the cherry tomatoes, sugar, onion,
garlic, oregano and stock into a saucepan,
bring to the boil and simmer for 15 minutes
over a low heat. Season to taste.
2 Meanwhile, cook the pasta in a large pan
of salted boiling water according to the packet
instructions.
3 Drain the pasta well, toss with the fresh
tomato sauce and, if using fresh oregano,
garnish with the extra.

• Per serving 343 kcalories, protein 12g, carbohydrate
73g, fat 2g, saturated fat none, fibre 4g, added sugar
1g, salt 0.13g

You'll find flat rice noodles with the oriental foods in the supermarket. Change the vegetables to suit your taste.

Zesty Noodle Stir Fry

140g/5oz flat rice noodles
6 tbsp soy sauce
5 tbsp fresh orange juice
½ tsp finely grated orange zest
1 tsp sugar
½ tsp cornflour
1 tbsp vegetable or sunflower oil
½ tbsp grated fresh ginger
2 garlic cloves, finely chopped
2 tbsp dry sherry
2 red peppers, seeded and sliced
2 carrots, cut into fine strips
2 courgettes, cut into fine strips
100g/4oz mangetout, sliced
220g can water chestnuts, sliced
1 bunch of spring onions, shredded

Takes 40 minutes • Serves 4
(easily halved)

1 Put the noodles in a large bowl, cover with boiling water for 4 minutes, then drain and rinse under cold running water.
2 Mix the soy sauce, orange juice and zest, sugar and cornflour. Heat the oil in a wok, add the ginger and garlic and fry for 1 minute. Add the sherry and peppers and fry for 1 minute. Add the carrots, courgettes and mangetout and fry for 3 minutes. Stir in the water chestnuts and spring onions and fry for 1 minute.
3 Add the soy sauce mix and noodles and stir fry until hot. Serve straight away.

• Per serving 240 kcalories, protein 6g, carbohydrate 47g, fat 3g, saturated fat none, fibre 4g, added sugar 1.6g, salt 2.77g

Use baby spinach
if you can't find rocket.

Mediterranean Spaghetti

140g/5oz spaghetti, snapped in half
2 tsp olive oil
250g pack cherry tomatoes, halved
1 large garlic clove, finely chopped
50g/2oz fresh rocket or
baby spinach leaves
handful of fresh basil leaves
125g pack 50% less fat mozzarella
cheese, drained and
finely chopped or grated

Takes 20–30 minutes • Serves 2

1 Cook the spaghetti in a large pan of salted boiling water for about 10 minutes, or according to the packet instructions, until just tender. Drain well and wipe out the pan.
2 Heat the oil in the pan, then tip in the tomatoes, garlic, rocket or spinach and basil. Season and stir over a medium heat until the leaves begin to wilt and the tomatoes look squashed.
3 Return the spaghetti to the pan and toss in the mozzarella over a low heat. When the spaghetti is hot and the mozzarella is melting, season and serve straight away. Don't let it stand or the cheese will go rubbery.

• Per serving 413 kcalories, protein 23g, carbohydrate 52g, fat 11g, saturated fat 5g, fibre 4g, added sugar none, salt 0.21g

This makes a great vegetarian family supper, but it can easily be halved to serve two.

Summer Veggie Pasta

200g/8oz farfalle (pasta bows)
175g/6oz fresh or frozen broad beans (about 650g/1lb 7oz in their pods)
1 tbsp good-quality olive oil
1 large onion, finely chopped
2 garlic cloves, chopped
2 large courgettes, cut into sticks
6 ripe plum tomatoes, cut into wedges
generous shot of Tabasco
handful of fresh basil, shredded

Takes 25–35 minutes • Serves 4

1 Cook the pasta in a large pan of salted boiling water according to the packet instructions, adding fresh broad beans for the last 3 minutes (frozen for the last 2 minutes).
2 While the pasta is cooking, heat the oil in a large frying pan and cook the onion over a medium heat for 1–2 minutes. Stir in the garlic and courgettes, toss over a medium heat for 2–3 minutes, then stir in the tomatoes and shake in the Tabasco. Stir for 2–3 minutes to soften the tomatoes a little (not too much or they will go mushy).
3 Drain the pasta and beans. Toss the courgette mixture and basil into the pasta and season. Serve in a large bowl.

• Per serving 284 kcalories, protein 12g, carbohydrate 51g, fat 5g, saturated fat 1g, fibre 7g, added sugar none, salt 0.1g

Transform this simple dish into a posh supper by adding thin slices
of smoked salmon with the peas, and substituting dill for the parsley.

Spaghetti with Peas and Parmesan

140g/5oz spaghetti
100g/4oz frozen petits pois or
garden peas
2 tsp olive oil
1 small onion, finely chopped
100g/4oz low-fat soft cheese with
chives and onion
finely grated zest of 1 lemon
3 tbsp freshly grated parmesan
cheese
1 tbsp chopped fresh flatleaf parsley

Takes 20–30 minutes • Serves 2

1 Cook the spaghetti in a large pan of salted
boiling water for 10–12 minutes, or according
to the packet instructions, until tender. Add
the peas for the last 2–3 minutes.
2 While the spaghetti is cooking, heat the oil
in a saucepan and fry the onion gently until
softened. Stir in the soft cheese and warm
it through, adding 3 tablespoons of the pasta
water to thin it down. Now stir in the lemon
zest and 2 tablespoons of the parmesan.
3 Drain the spaghetti and peas really well,
return them to the pan and gently stir in the
sauce. Season, then pile into serving bowls
and sprinkle the parsley and remaining
parmesan over the top.

• Per serving 420 kcalories, protein 22g, carbohydrate
61g, fat 11g, saturated fat 3g, fibre 5g, added sugar
none, salt 0.83g

Vary the flavours of this aromatic dish by using basil instead of coriander, and cooked chicken instead of prawns.

Chinese Noodles with Spicy Prawns

2 tbsp olive oil
1 medium onion, roughly chopped
1 rounded tbsp coriander purée
(from a tube)
pinch of chilli flakes, or to taste
400g can chopped tomatoes
with garlic
1 rounded tbsp tomato purée
1 tbsp vegetable bouillon powder
½ × 250g pack Chinese egg noodles
400g/14oz cooked peeled frozen
prawns (large North Atlantic
ones are tender and juicy)

Takes 30–40 minutes • Serves 4

1 Heat the oil in a wok and stir fry the onion, coriander purée and chilli for 5 minutes until the onion is softened. Pour in the tomatoes and 1½ canfuls hot water, add the tomato purée and sprinkle over the bouillon powder. Season well. Bring to a bubble, stirring, then simmer for 15 minutes.

2 While the sauce is simmering, break the noodles into a bowl and pour in enough boiling water to cover. Stir and set aside.

3 When the sauce is ready, drain the noodles and tip them into the sauce with the frozen prawns. Stir well and heat through for 2 minutes only – just to defrost and heat the prawns. Taste for seasoning and add more chilli if you like.

• Per serving 311 kcalories, protein 29g, carbohydrate 29g, fat 10g, saturated fat 1g, fibre 2g, added sugar none, salt 4.76g

You could use spinach leaves or shredded, leftover cooked Brussels sprouts instead of the chard in this recipe.

Good-for-you Pasta

150ml/¼ pint tomato sauce (homemade or from a jar)
350g/12oz pasta ribbons, such as pappardelle
175g/6oz cauliflower, cut into bite-sized florets
175g/6oz broccoli, cut into bite-sized florets
120g pack baby chard
a little olive oil
freshly grated parmesan cheese, to serve

Takes 50 minutes • Serves 4

1 First purée the tomato sauce, if it is not already smooth.
2 Bring a large pan of salted water to the boil and cook the pasta for 8–10 minutes, or according to the packet instructions, until just tender.
3 Meanwhile, cook the cauliflower in another pan for 6 minutes, add the broccoli and cook for a further 3–4 minutes, until both are just tender. Drain well and keep warm. Heat the tomato sauce through.
4 Drain the pasta and stir in the chard with a little olive oil and seasoning. Toss in the broccoli, cauliflower and hot tomato sauce and serve with parmesan.

• Per serving 498 kcalories, protein 20g, carbohydrate 99g, fat 5g, saturated fat 1g, fibre 9g, added sugar 1g, salt 0.72g

If you have a nut allergy,
replace the almonds with pine nuts.

15-minute Chicken Pasta

350g/12oz farfalle (pasta bows)
300g/10oz broccoli,
cut into small florets
1 tbsp olive oil
3 large skinless boneless chicken
breasts, cut into
bite-sized chunks
2 garlic cloves, crushed
2 tbsp wholegrain mustard
juice of 1 large or 2 small oranges
25g/1oz flaked almonds, toasted

Takes 15 minutes • Serves 4

1 Cook the pasta in a large pan of salted boiling water for 8–10 minutes, or according to the packet instructions, until tender. Three minutes before the pasta is cooked, throw in the broccoli and continue to boil.

2 While the pasta is cooking, gently heat the oil in a large frying pan or wok and fry the chicken, stirring occasionally, until cooked and golden, about 5–7 minutes, adding the garlic for the last 2 minutes.

3 Mix the mustard with the orange juice in a small bowl. Pour the mixture over the chicken and simmer gently for a minute or two.

4 Drain the pasta and broccoli, reserving 3 tablespoons of the water. Toss the pasta and broccoli with the chicken, stir in the water and almonds, and season well before serving.

• Per serving 531 kcalories, protein 43g, carbohydrate 70g, fat 11g, saturated fat 1g, fibre 6g, added sugar none, salt 0.52g

Hot-smoked salmon usually comes ready-flaked in tubs or vacuum-packed as steaks. It has a juicy texture and delicious smoky flavour.

Spaghetti with Salmon and Peas

400g/14oz spaghetti
100g/4oz frozen petits pois
150–160g pack hot-smoked salmon,
flaked into bite-sized chunks
20g pack fresh dill, roughly chopped
(tough stalks removed)
3 rounded tbsp crème fraîche

Takes 20 minutes • Serves 4

1 Cook the spaghetti at a rolling boil in salted water, stirring occasionally to keep the strands separate, until the pasta is just tender but with a bite. Check the cooking time on the packet, as it does vary. When the pasta is almost done, throw in the peas.
2 Reserve about 4 tablespoons of the pasta water, then drain the pasta and peas and return them to the pan with the reserved water.
3 Set the pan over a very low heat and toss in the salmon, dill, crème fraîche and seasoning. Heat through briefly, then serve.

• Per serving 470 kcalories, protein 24g, carbohydrate 77g, fat 10g, saturated fat 4g, fibre 4g, added sugar none, salt 1.85g

A great storecupboard standby that's brimming with goodness and is a great family favourite.

Minestrone Pasta Pot

2 tbsp olive oil
1 small onion, finely chopped
2 tbsp tomato purée
300g/10oz frozen mixed vegetables
(including peas, sweetcorn,
carrots and broccoli, but not
the chunky stewpacks)
700ml/1¼ pints hot vegetable stock
175g/6oz small pasta shapes,
such as conchigliette
220g can baked beans
grated cheddar cheese, to serve

Takes 25–35 minutes • Serves 4

1 Heat the olive oil in a saucepan over a medium heat and gently fry the onion for a few minutes until it starts to soften. Stir in the tomato purée, then tip in the frozen vegetables and pour in the stock.
2 Bring to the boil, add the pasta and stir. Cover and simmer for 12–14 minutes or until the pasta is cooked.
3 Stir in the beans and heat through, then taste for seasoning. Serve hot, with a bowl of grated cheddar for sprinkling over the top.

• Per serving 294 kcalories, protein 11g, carbohydrate 49g, fat 7g, saturated fat 1g, fibre 4g, added sugar 2g, salt 1.58g

If you love garlic, add a couple of chopped cloves with the breadcrumbs.

Broccoli and Anchovy Spaghetti

350g/12oz spaghetti
350g/12oz broccoli
5 tbsp olive oil
6 canned anchovy fillets,
drained and chopped
2 fresh red chillies, seeded and
finely chopped
100g/4oz white breadcrumbs,
made with stale bread

Takes 25–30 minutes • Serves 4

1 Cook the spaghetti in a large pan of salted boiling water for 10–12 minutes, or according to the packet instructions, until tender. Cut the broccoli into small florets, thinly slice the thick stalks and throw into the pan of pasta for the last 3 minutes.

2 Meanwhile, heat 3 tablespoons of the oil in a frying pan, add the anchovies and chillies and fry briefly. Add the breadcrumbs and cook, stirring, for about 5 minutes until the crumbs are crunchy and golden.

3 Drain the spaghetti and broccoli and return to the pan. Toss with three quarters of the crumb mixture, some seasoning and the remaining oil. Serve sprinkled with the remaining crumbs.

• Per serving 400 kcalories, protein 17g, carbohydrate 78g, fat 4g, saturated fat 0.5g, fibre 5g, added sugar none, salt 0.8g

This light and elegant dish is ideal
for midweek entertaining.

Chilli Prawn Linguine

280g/10oz linguine
200g/8oz sugar snap peas, trimmed
2 tbsp olive oil
2 large garlic cloves, finely chopped
1 large fresh red chilli, seeded and
finely chopped
24 peeled raw king prawns,
12 cherry tomatoes, halved
handful of fresh basil leaves
salad leaves, to serve

FOR THE LIME DRESSING
2 tbsp virtually fat-free fromage frais
grated zest and juice of 2 limes
2 tsp golden caster sugar

Takes 25–30 minutes • Serves 6

1 Mix the dressing ingredients in a small bowl,
season and set aside.
2 Cook the pasta according to the packet
instructions. Add the sugar snap peas for the
last minute or so of the cooking time.
3 Meanwhile, heat the oil in a wok or large
frying pan, toss in the garlic and chilli and cook
over a fairly gentle heat for about 30 seconds.
Add the prawns and cook over a high heat,
stirring frequently, for about 3 minutes until
they turn pink. Add the tomatoes and cook,
stirring occasionally, for 3 minutes until they
start to soften. Drain the pasta and sugar
snaps well, then toss into the prawn mixture.
Tear in the basil leaves, stir and season.
4 Serve with salad leaves drizzled with the
lime dressing.

• Per serving 333 kcalories, protein 32g, carbohydrate
42g, fat 5g, saturated fat 1g, fibre 3g, added sugar 2g,
salt 0.9g

Index